Irish Narrow Gauge Railways

A VIEW FROM THE PAST

MICHAEL H. C. BAKER

Ian Allan
PUBLISHING

Front cover:
An unidentified County Donegal Railways 4-6-4T at Barnesmore Gap, between Stranorlar and Donegal Town. *P. B. Whitehouse*

Back cover:
No 8 leaving Annascaul, on the Tralee & Dingle Railway, with steam to spare, 29 June 1951. *Author's collection*

Title page:
Ballycastle station on 18 April 1948 with Compound 2-4-2T No 43 leaving for Ballymoney. *H. C. Casserley*

Top Left:
Ballycastle Railway 4-4-2T as NCC No 114 poses for the camera in 1931. *LPC*

Left:
Clougher Valley Railway's No 6 *Erne* stands at Fivemiletown on 25 June 1937. *H. C. Casserley*

Note: The maps are not reproduced to scale and only show selected stations or stopping points.

First published 1999

ISBN 0 7110 2680 7

© Michael H. C. Baker 1999

Published by Ian Allan Publishing

an imprint of Ian Allan Publishing Ltd, Terminal House, Shepperton, Surrey TW17 8AS.

Printed by Ian Allan Printing Ltd, Riverdene Business Park, Hersham, Surrey KT12 4RG.

Code: 9910/B1

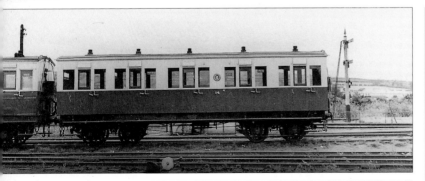

Above:
County Donegal Railways' five compartment bogie coach No 14 seen at Strabane on 23 June 1937. *H. C. Casserley*

Contents

Acknowledgements

I am grateful to a number of friends in Ireland although, of course, any mistakes and omissions are entirely my responsibility. Much of the information on the long-vanished industrial railways I have culled from a copy of Walter McGrath's *Some Industrial Railways of Ireland*, published in Cork in 1959, a copy of which was sent me by Tim Moriarty, the long-serving librarian of the Irish Railway Record Society. It is also to the IRRS I owe thanks for organising visits to both Shanes Castle and Stradbally, a good few years ago now, where I was able to ride behind two of the three delightful little former Bord na Móna Andrew Barclay 0-4-0WTs. On another IRRS outing I rode in a preserved County Donegal railcar alongside the River Foyle from the splendid North West of Ireland Railway Society museum at Londonderry. My thanks go to Society member Arthur Thompson of Derry, for keeping me up to date with progress at the museum and for the latest information on other narrow gauge preservation schemes in County Donegal and elsewhere in the north of Ireland. All interested in railway preservation in Ireland remain in debt to many others, their names often forgotten, who helped save from oblivion various narrow gauge artefacts, often back in the dark days when revival of the narrow gauge in any form other than within the pages of books and magazines seemed impossible. Finally, no praise is too high for the National Railway Museum at Cultra, which displays so much of what has survived of the narrow gauge in its wonderful purpose-built setting beside the historic waters of Belfast Lough.

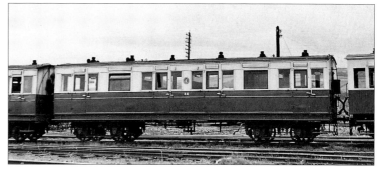

Below left:
Stranorlar, on the County Donegal Railways, on 7 August 1930 with No 14 *Erne* awaiting departure for Strabane. *H. C. Casserley*

Top Right:
County Donegal Railways' No 28, seen at Strabane on 23 June 1937. *H. C. Casserley*

Centre Right:
Londonderry & Lough Swilly Railway No 12 standing outside Letterkenny engine shed in September 1948. The truck in the centre is standing on the connecting line to the County Donegal Railways. *O. H. Prosser*

Below:
The Arigna branch of the Cavan & Leitrim with ex-Tralee & Dingle No 3 in charge. *P. B. Whitehouse*

Introduction

I write this aboard the Belfast-bound 'Enterprise' north of Dundalk, as a grey dawn breaks over the Border, although further north there are pink-tinged hints of something better.

What, you may ask, does this have to do with the narrow gauge? Well for one thing I am on my way to the Transport Museum at Cultra. I have visited a good few museums in various parts of the world and there is none finer than Northern Ireland's national one beside the historic waters of Belfast Lough. We waited a very long time for it but the wait was certainly worth while. Costing £1.9 million, the highly imaginative building, displaying the exhibits to the best possible advantage, was funded by the Department of Education for Northern Ireland although it covers the whole 32 counties. Much of what is there used to be at Witham Street in the city, tightly packed together, but safe and reasonably accessible. Some items had been there a very long time. Long enough for the far-seeing curators to have rescued an astonishing collection of artefacts from the narrow gauge as it closed down all over Ireland in the years immediately after World War 2. My only complaint is that it has serious need of a proper guidebook detailing all its wonderful exhibits.

In the main the photographs in this book, many of them previously unpublished, are from the Ian Allan archives, taken by a handful of Irish, Scottish and English enthusiasts when the narrow gauge was part of everyday life for many. The narrow gauge was mostly to be found in the more remote parts of the country, although it also existed, in one form or another, in or near Cork, Limerick, Dublin, Newry, Larne and Derry.

Our story would be less than complete if we did not bring it up to date. In doing so we arrive at what is perhaps the most astonishing part, a coda not even the most optimistic could have anticipated back in 1961 when the last narrow gauge trains ran, on the West Clare. Yet as we enter a new millennium there are narrow gauge railways either at work or under construction in various parts of Ireland, north and south of the Border, and a number of museums telling the continuing story.

Skimming down from the border, I always make a point of looking down from the great

Below:
County Donegal Railways 2-6-4T No 19 *Letterkenny* at Strabane in 1931.
Real Photos

18-arch Craigmore Viaduct on to the trackbed of the Bessbrook & Newry Tramway. This closed in 1948 but the Transport Museum has No 2, one of the original Bessbrook & Newry cars of 1885. Well, not quite original. The chassis and driving cab certainly are, but the passenger accommodation is a Dublin & Lucan body, grafted on in 1942. After closure, the tram was returned to Manchester, whence both had originated, and became a cricket pavilion. Just why it was considered worth while shipping these ancient remains across the Irish Sea is not recorded. By the 1940s it had become the oldest working tram anywhere in these islands, so perhaps its historic significance was recognised. It had clearly found its sea legs, for five years later it made the return voyage and was restored by the museum. While not very pretty, it is a marvel, simply on account of still being in existence.

The contrast in the interior of Bessbrook & Newry No 2 and the French-built luxury of the 1996-vintage 'Enterprise' carriages used on the Dublin–Belfast run is as great as that between the homes of most inhabitants of either Bessbrook or Newry in the 1880s and those of their descendants 110 years later. Three pretty girls in their late teens get in at Newry, off for a day's shopping in Belfast, and sit opposite lucky me.

Cultra is on the Bangor line and the sunshine which breaks through as we draw into Belfast Central tempts me into visiting the seaside at Bangor, a well set up, prosperous little town, before heading back to renew acquaintance with old friends at the Transport Museum. Much the best represented narrow gauge system, at Cultra and elsewhere, is the County Donegal. Sadly, the other Donegal narrow gauge company, the Londonderry & Lough Swilly, has very little to show for its 100 years of railway operation — other than the fact that it is still in business! The County Donegal lasted until 1959, which partly explains why so much of it remains, but the LLSR began to invest in buses in 1929. It very quickly built up a fleet of nearly 40 vehicles, and rail services were much reduced. One of the Lough Swilly's problems was that its stations were often several miles from the communities they served; the bus, of course, could drive right down the main street.

When I first visited County Donegal in 1978, it was easy to make out much of the Lough Swilly's trackbed in various parts of the county, and there were even a few old carriage bodies either still in use as stores or fairly recently abandoned. I also came across, and indeed travelled upon, some of the long-lived batch of Leyland Royal Tiger buses, dating from 1951-3, which replaced the service.

But the Lough Swilly soldiers on and still, remarkably, calls itself a railway company, making it one of the longest-lived transport organisations in the British Isles. You can even buy a scale model of one of its buses, the only mass-produced model of an Irish narrow gauge vehicle — even if it is standard bus width! But then it could come as quite a shock on first encountering the narrow gauge to discover that on many lines the carriages were little smaller than standard gauge ones. Some narrow gauge lines, the County Donegal for instance, operated carriages which were designed along similar lines to standard gauge ones, with separate compartments, and ran either on six wheels or on four-wheel bogies, but others employed tramlike vehicles, some with American-style end verandas. The Londonderry & Lough Swilly belonged to the first category; other Northern Ireland lines, the Clogher Valley for example, the latter.

The locomotives could be a surprise too. Brought up on miniature gauge lines such as that which used to employ GWR-style 4-4-0s running around Chessington Zoo, or the Romney, Hythe & Dymchurch Pacifics, the boilers of which one could comfortably peer over, I found Irish narrow gauge tank engines towered over me.

This book records the fact that a surprising amount of the narrow gauge remains, or is being revived, but pride of place in keeping it going must go to Bord Na Móna, or the Irish Peat Commission. Founded in 1946, it laid 3ft gauge tracks to connect its bogs with works, power stations and factories. At the last count it possessed the extraordinary total of around 1,200 miles of track, far and away the largest railway system in Ireland and the largest industrial railway system in Europe. Visitors can enjoy this aspect of the narrow gauge in Ireland today by taking a trip on the Bord Na Móna's Clanmacnoise & West Offaly Railway at Shannonbridge, not far from Athlone.

Left:
The newest narrow gauge steam locomotives were three 0-4-0WTs built by Andrew Barclay to work on the Bord Na Móna peat bogs in 1949. Although they lasted only four years with their original owners, all found later employment. No 1 was rebuilt as a 2ft 3in gauge 0-4-2T by the Talyllyn in North Wales. No 2 is seen here at Stradbally in County Laois, with plenty of members of the Irish Railway Record Society assisting the driver on an outing in the 1980s. *Author*

Below:
Considering the little 0-4-0WTs originally ran over the wide open spaces of the peat bogs, it is curious that the two which stayed in Ireland later found homes deep in the woods. No 3 is seen here at Lord O'Neil's Shanes Castle Railway in 1985. Its two carriages were originally Belgian tramcars. They have moved on to the hopefully revived Giant's Causeway scheme in County Antrim. *Author*

1. Londonderry & Lough Swilly Railway

Possibly the most remarkable thing about this company, whose network was once almost as extensive as the County Donegal, is that it is still in existence. The LLSR began to run bus services in the late 1920s and this has ensured its survival after the last train ran in August 1953.

As with the County Donegal it began as a 5ft 3in gauge line, the first section from Londonderry to Farland Point on Lough Swilly and Buncrana opening in November 1863. The Farland line lasted for only three years, becoming redundant once the steamer services were transferred to Fahan Pier on the Buncrana line. A narrow gauge line from Tooban Junction to Letterkenny was opened in June 1883 and two years later the original section of the Londonderry & Lough Swilly was converted to the 3ft gauge.

In July 1901 the most northerly stretch of railway in Ireland came into existence when the extension from Buncrana up towards Malin Head, terminating at Carndonagh, was opened. In the far west of Donegal the line from Letterkenny to Burtonport completed the system in March 1903.

The Lough Swilly owned some fine locomotives, including the most powerful (and the only eight-coupled) narrow gauge engines in the country, indeed anywhere in the British Isles, in the shape of two Hudswell Clarke 4-8-4Ts of 1912 and two 4-8-0s of 1905. They were excellent machines. Sadly no LLSR locomotives have survived; all had been cut up by 1954, a few years before the preservation movement had got properly into its stride. The Buncrana to Carndonagh line closed in October 1935; the Londonderry to Buncrana line to passengers in September 1948 and to goods in August 1953. The Gweedore to Burtonport section closed in June 1940 although wartime shortages of oil for the replacement road vehicles saw most of it revived between 1941 and its final closure in 1947; that from Letterkenny to Gweedore closed in June 1947. The last sections between Derry and Letterkenny closed in August 1953.

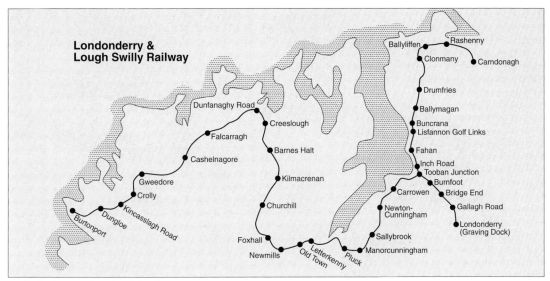

Top Left:
The Graving Dock station, the Lough Swilly's Londonderry terminus, in 1933. In an article published in the February 1919 *Railway Magazine* the author wrote, 'The necessity for new station premises at Londonderry is urgent. The facilities now existing… are totally inadequate as regards accommodation: the present passenger station is insanitary, a disgrace both to the railway and the City of Londonderry.' Despite these words there had been virtually no improvement in the intervening years. A 4-6-2T is about to depart with the stock of a Sunday excursion. *LGRP*

Centre Left:
Pennyburn, the headquarters of the Londonderry & Lough Swilly Railway, in 1933. To the right is the station, while behind the two 4-6-2Ts is the engine shed. *LGRP*

Below:
Hudswell Clarke 4-6-2T No 8 shunting at Londonderry Docks, 24 August 1951.
Ian Allan Library

Top Right:
No 2, one of the four Andrew Barclay 4-6-0Ts of 1902, shunting at Letterkenny c1948. A passenger brake serves as the goods brake van, typical LLSR practice. No 2 lasted until the end of rail services, being broken up in 1953.
Ian Allan Library

Centre Right:
Horsebox No 62, Londonderry, 1933. It bears the initials of the Letterkenny & Burtonport Extension Railway but this did not preclude its use over all sections of the LLSR.
LGRP

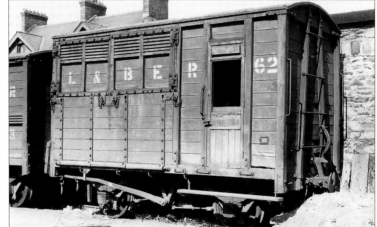

Bottom Right:
One of six oil tankers which worked on the Lough Swilly system. The Anglo-American Oil Company (Pratts Spirit) would later become Esso.
LGRP

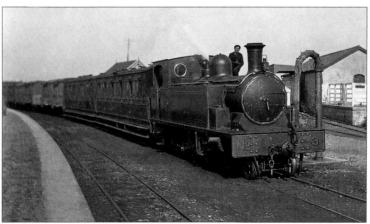

Top Left:
1902-built 4-6-0T No 3 stands at Tooban Junction, 14 June 1952. *A. F. Porter*

Bottom Left:
4-6-0T No 3 at Letterkenny with a mixed train from Burtonport, May 1939. *Real Photographs*

Top Right:
No 12, one of the two Hudswell Clarke 4-8-0s of 1905, about to set off from Burtonport with a mixed train on a sunny June day in 1937. These two sisters were the only narrow gauge tender engines in Ireland and, along with the tank engine version, Nos 5 and 6, the most powerful. Indeed, eight-coupled engines were exceedingly rare in Ireland, the only others being two short-lived 4-8-0T shunters built at Inchicore for the GSWR. *H. C. Casserley*

Centre Right:
Fahan Pier, 9¼ miles northwest of Londonderry on the Carndonagh line, with the abandoned LLSR steamer *Lake of Shadows* drawn up on the beach. It was scrapped in 1934. *LGRP*

Bottom Right:
Rathmullan Pier with the LLSR offices (or hut!) where one could buy tickets for the steamer service to Fahan and Rathmelton. *LGRP*

Top Left:
Ballyliffin, two stops short of the terminus of the Carndonagh branch and very nearly the most northerly station in Ireland, in 1931, four years before closure. The locomotive at the head of its three-coach train is one of the Hudswell Clarke 4-6-2Ts of 1899. *LGRP*

Centre Left:
The terminus of the Lough Swilly's line north from Tooban Junction was Carndonagh. More than 40 years after the last train had called, the station stands intact with a Lough Swilly bus, one of 11 ex-CIE 'E' class Leopards transferred to the LLSR in 1973, in the yard; August 1978. *Author*

Below:
Kilmacrenan station on the Burtonport line in the summer of 1931. No 13, one of the Hawthorn Leslie 4-6-2Ts of 1910, is about to set off with a Burtonport train. *LGRP*

Top Right:
A picture taken on the same day, this time of an up, Letterkenny-bound, mixed train in the charge of 4-8-0 No 12. Note the County Donegal van standing on the down platform beside the locomotive. *LGRP*

Centre Right:
Cresslough station with one of the 4-6-2Ts of 1910 on a mixed train, seen from the south. *LGRP*

Below:
Buncrana, the terminus of the line from Tooban Junction from 1935 onwards. Beyond is Lough Swilly. 4-6-2T No 10 stands with a Londonderry train on 19 April 1948. Just visible on the platform, between the leading carriage and the station building, is a Lough Swilly bus, a Leyland 'TS3' Tiger dating from 1933 and fitted with locally-built Catherwood body. This would have served the peninsular area up towards Malin Head, abandoned by the railway in 1935. *H. C. Casserley*

Above:
No 13 seen on arrival at Burtonport, journey's end, with its mixed train of two bogie carriages and five wagons in 1931. *LGRP*

Below:
No 29, an LLSR five-compartment, six-wheel third. *H. C. Casserley*

Above:
A six-compartment third, bearing the initials of the Letterkenny & Burtonport Extension Railway, in 1937.
H. C. Casserley

Below:
For a time in the 1970s, preservationists established a centre at the former County Donegal station at Victoria Road, Derry. One exhibit was this rather worse for wear but basically intact LLSR carriage body, rescued from Pennyburn. A five-compartment third dating from 1885, rebuilt in 1922, it has been restored by Enterprise Ulster and is now awaiting an underframe. *Author*

Above:
Rather less happy is the fate of this LLSR carriage slowly disintegrating and disappearing into the undergrowth.
Author

Centre Left:
Mixed gauge track in Londonderry Docks.
Author

Bottom Left:
A pair of CIE-built 'E' class Leyland Leopards outside the former County Donegal station, Letterkenny, August 1978, the one in the foreground having been transferred to Lough Swilly. The further one, still with CIE, bearing a rather ironic advert, is operating a former County Donegal route.
Author

2. County Donegal Railway

Perhaps the best loved of all the Irish narrow gauge systems, the County Donegal began life as the 5ft 3in gauge Finn Valley Railway between Strabane and Stranorlar in September 1863. In April 1882 the 3ft gauge West Donegal opened between Stranorlar and Druminin, and to Donegal Town seven years later. A line from Donegal to Killybegs was opened in August 1893 and one from Stranorlar to Glenties in July, 1895. Meanwhile in 1892 the Finn Valley and the West Donegal Railways amalgamated to form the Donegal Railway Company.

As the future of railways in that part of Ireland clearly lay with the narrow gauge, the Finn Valley was converted to 3ft over the weekend of 13-15 July 1894. Further extensions

brought the 3ft gauge from Strabane to Derry in August 1900, from Donegal to Ballyshannon in September 1905 and, finally, from Strabane to Letterkenny in January 1909. The system now had a route mileage of 124½ making it the largest in the country.

On 1 May 1906 the County Donegal became the joint property of the Great Northern and the English Midland Railway (although the 1909 addition of the Strabane & Letterkenny Railway was nominally independent), and from then on was managed as the County Donegal Railways Joint Committee. A world pioneer in petrol and diesel railcars under the remarkable Henry Forbes, who was in charge from 1910 to 1943, the County Donegal also possessed a fleet of

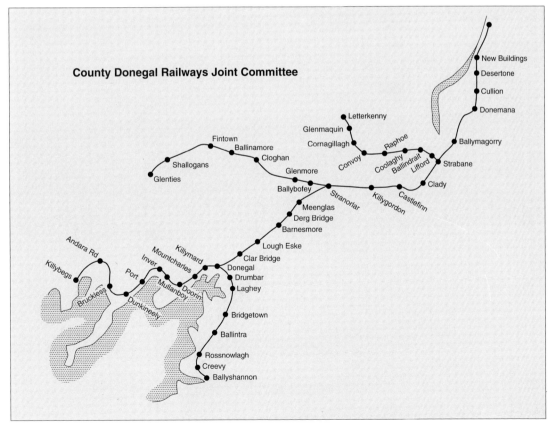

County Donegal Railways Joint Committee

fine steam locomotives. It began operating petrol railcars in the 1920s, and the first diesel railcar in the British Isles was put to work on the County Donegal in 1931. But not even the County Donegal could resist the all-conquering car, bus and lorry, and it closed down on 31 December 1959. However, far more of the County Donegal has been preserved than of practically all the other narrow gauge lines put together and it is still possible to ride in County Donegal vehicles in the northwest of Ireland.

An American bought up a large amount of County Donegal rolling stock, intending to ship it across the Atlantic, while two of its most modern railcars were sold to the Isle of Man Railway. In the event nothing went to America. Some rotted away, other items were kept under cover or went on display at the railway museum in Belfast. In 1989 the North West of Ireland Railway Society opened a magnificent brick-built museum in Derry, built for it by Derry City Council, on the trackbed of the GNR line immediately south of the River Foyle

Bridge, containing a collection of County Donegal and other narrow gauge artefacts. At the same time track was laid alongside the River Foyle and this currently extends some two miles. Two railcars, Nos 12 and 18, which had been kept under cover, have since operated regularly on it. No 12, a 41-seat GNR/Walker Bros vehicle dating from 1934, has just had £60,000 spent on it. In your author's humble opinion, a ride on this is a good deal more exciting than many a journey behind preserved steam. Elsewhere, nearly two miles of track has been relaid between Fintown and Glenties by the South Donegal Preservation Group and diesel-hauled trains are operated, while there is another museum devoted to the CDR at Donegal Town station which has been renovated by the County Donegal Railway Restoration Society. All this has meant that much more remains of the County Donegal than any other Irish narrow gauge railway. As it was the largest and perhaps the best loved, this is only fitting.

DONEGAL RAILWAY.

General Manager: R. H. LIVESEY, Esq.
Secretary: W. R. LAWSON, Esq.
All trains 1, 2 & 3 class.
[AUG 1900]

(timetable showing DOWN and UP services for week-days and week-day[s] between Strabane, Clady, Castlefinn, Liscooly, Killygordon, Stranorlar, Glenmore, Cloghan, Ballinamore, Fintown, Glenties, Meen Glas, Barnesmore, Lough Eske, Donegal, Killymard, Mountcharles, Dooran Road, Inver, Port, Dunkineely, Bruckless, Ardara Road, Killybegs, and return via Mountcharles fairs & Donegal fairs from Stranorlar)

* Stops as may be required on notice to the guard at preceding stopping station..

TOURISTS for CLENGARRIFF and KILLARNEY should ask for the CIRCULAR TOUR TICKETS BY THE "PRINCE OF WALES' ROUTE," applicable via MALLOW, or via CORK and BANTRY. THROUGH BOOKINGS from most English and Irish Railways. Literature sent post free on application to the General Manager. TELEGRAPHIC ADDRESS—"CROKER, CORK."

Left
Timetable for the period commencing August 1900.
Paul Collins collection

Below Left:
Strabane was one of the most interesting railway locations in Ireland, as this picture shows, for it was here that one could watch two of the best run railways in the country, the County Donegal and the Great Northern, going about their business and often transferring it from one to the other. On the left Donegal Nasmyth Wilson 4-6-4T No 11 *Erne* of Class 4, dating from 1904, has charge of a goods train bound for Stranorlar, while GNR 4-4-0 No 43 acts as station pilot on the far right; 2 October 1958.
J.G. Dewing

Top Right:
It is no exaggeration to state that the County Donegal was one of the most important pioneers of petrol and diesel traction in Europe. It owned 21, brought into service between 1906 and 1951. One from the middle period was No 6. A view of the interior is seen here when new at Strabane in 1930. No 6 was a 32hp petrol-engined vehicle, the mechanical section being built at the GNR's Dundalk Works, the body by O'Doherty of Strabane. *Ian Allan Library*

Right:
It would be stretching a point to claim that all County Donegal railcars were of uniformly handsome appearance. No 8, another GNR/O'Doherty vehicle, dating from 1931, pokes its snout in the direction of a four-wheel van at Strabane, watched by the shunter and friend with trilby hat, 20 April 1948. *H. C. Casserley*

Below Right:
Of rather better proportions was No 10, seen here at Ballyshannon on 11 May 1950. This was a Gardner-engined 74hp car, built by Walker Bros in 1932 for the Clogher Valley Railway, and was the first articulated power bogie railcar to run in the country. It came to the County Donegal after the closure of the Clogher Valley in 1942 and is now in the Railway Museum at Cultra. *W. A. Camwell*

Bottom Right:
Although railcars played an increasing part in handling passenger traffic on the County Donegal, there was still a place for steam, on excursions and fairs traffic in particular. No 15 *Mourne*, a Nasmyth Wilson 4-6-4T of 1904, stands at Victoria Road, Derry, 23 June 1937. *H. C. Casserley*

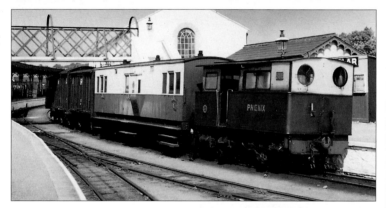

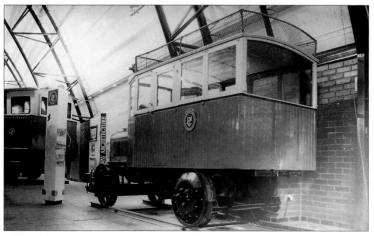

Top Left:
No 16, a GNR/Walker railcar of 1936, at the County Donegal station, Letterkenny, May 1957. The Londonderry & Lough Swilly station was alongside the Donegal's to the south.
J. G. Dewing

Left:
No 4 *Meenglas*, a Nasmyth Wilson 2-6-4T of 1907, at Killygordon with the 10.45am Stranorlar-Strabane goods, 6 August 1959. Passenger carriages were used as goods brake vans; the company was happy to convey passengers if they appeared. *K. R. Pirt*

Below Left:
Among the most interesting of all County Donegal motive power was No 11 *Phoenix*, seen here at Stranorlar. Originally an Atkinson-Walker steam-powered tractor of the Clogher Valley Railway, it was bought by the Donegal in 1929 and rebuilt as a diesel at Dundalk. It then served as a shunter until the end of the County Donegal, when it passed into honourable retirement at the Belfast Transport Museum
P. Ransome-Wallis

Bottom Left:
The County Donegal's first railcar, No 1. This little 4-wheeler was built by Allday & Onions of Birmingham in 1907, a 10-seat vehicle, originally of only 10hp but seen here as preserved in the Belfast Transport Museum with the 36hp Ford engine fitted in 1949. This historic vehicle paved the way for the subsequent highly successful fleet of railcars introduced by the County Donegal. Although of very limited capacity, in its final form it was capable of hauling a trailer and worked on the Finn Valley section. It ran 19,457 miles in its long career. Upon withdrawal in 1956 it was presented to the Belfast Museum. *Author*

Right:
Perhaps the most celebrated location on the County Donegal was the remote, windswept Barnesmore Gap between Stranorlar and Donegal Town. The trackbed can still be traced easily beside the road which finally killed off the railway. Struggling through the Gap is a mixed train, the leading three carriages being very special. They were built by the NCC in Belfast in 1928 for the Ballymena-Larne boat trains. They were virtually of broad gauge dimensions, two of them being 52ft 4ins long over buffers, and all three had corridor connections and electric lighting. The County Donegal bought them after the Ballycastle line closed in 1950. *P. B. Whitehouse*

Below:
A view of the bridge under which the train in the previous picture is about to pass, taken some 30 years later. *Author*

Above:
Railcar No 12 being turned on the turntable at Donegal Town on a sunny summer afternoon in 1950. *S. H. Keyse*

Below:
Since the closure of the County Donegal, railcar No 12 has had an adventurous career. It helped in the demolition of much of the railway's network and was then stored, under cover fortunately, at Stranorlar. In 1972 the North West of Ireland Railway Society took over the still surviving Londonderry Victoria Road station, which then belonged to a firm of wholesale grocers. The manager, Frederick Towers, had been sympathetic to the idea of preservation and his successor, James Devine, gave permission for part of the station to be used as a museum. This opened in June 1972 and No 12 was bought and, still in working order, was used to give rides over a short length of track. Sadly the museum had to be abandoned but Lord O'Neil gave the exhibits a home at his Shanes Castle Railway beside Lough Neagh, where No 12 is seen in 1980. *Author*

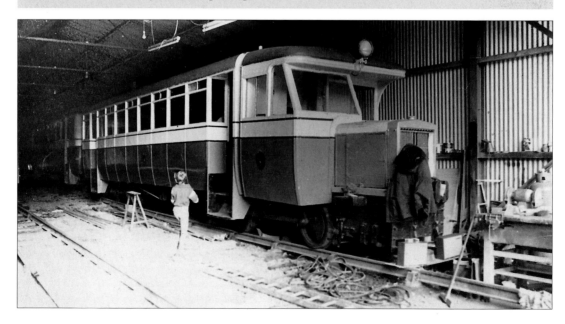

Above:
One of the steam locomotives which survived the closure of the County Donegal was 2-6-4T No 6 *Columbkille*. It is seen here at Victoria Road, Derry, in August 1978.
Author

Right:
Another is No 4 *Meenglas*, seen here cosmetically restored at the North West of Ireland Museum on the west bank of the Foyle at Londonderry.
Author

Above:
No 6 *Columbkille* in steam behind No 2 *Blanche* at Victoria Road, Derry, some 30 years earlier. The pair are about to set off for Strabane after bringing in a Whit Monday special. *N. W. Sprinks*

Left:
A general view of Donegal station on 11 May 1950. There are three railcars on view, one attached to a red van. There were 23 of these lightly constructed wagons, designed to be towed by railcars and painted red to distinguish them. *W. A. Camwell*

Above:
Conversation piece at
Ballyshannon on 11 May 1950.
Gardner-engined railcar
No 10, built for the Clogher
Valley Railway in 1932, has
charge of a trailer and a red
van. *W. A. Camwell*

Right:
A GNR/Walker railcar with
two red vans on a Donegal-
Ballyshannon working.
P. B. Whitehouse

Above:
Walker railcar No 15 of 1936 approaching Ballyshannon on a working from Donegal Town, 19 July 1957. *C. P. Boocock*

Below:
There seems to be plenty of work for 2-6-4T No 2 *Blanche*, judging by the length of its train, as it pauses at Raphoe with the 12.25pm Letterkenny-Strabane on 7 August 1959 but the missing track and overgrown state of the near platform suggest that the good times are long past. *K. R. Pirt*

Above:
Maintenance work at Stranorlar, in the summer of 1956. *Ian Allan Library*

Right:
After the County Donegal closed down, much of its rolling stock was bought with the intention of shipping it to the USA. In this view of Strabane on 6 August 1964, two Class 5 2-6-4Ts, No 5 *Drumboe* and No 4 *Meenglas* are seen with a number of carriages in the distance, while ex-GNR 'U' class 4-4-0 *Meath* takes water while working the 10.15 Londonderry to Belfast. In fact none of these locomotives or carriages ever did cross the Atlantic but continued for decades to succumb gradually to the elements and other depredations until some were rescued and brought to Derry. *Noel A. Machell*

3. Clogher Valley Railway

Opened in May 1887 this roadside line was 37 miles long. Occasionally it left the roadside and headed across fields. These diversions necessitated cattle grids, which are said to have been invented by the Clogher Valley Railway. In contrast, at Caledon and at Fivemiletown it ran down the middle of the main streets.

It connected two GNR stations, Tynan on the Clones to Armagh line and Maguiresbridge on the Clones to Enniskillen line. Four mixed trains ran daily in each direction and took roughly three hours to complete their journey; accurate timekeeping was not a forte of the Clogher Valley. In 1894 it changed its legal

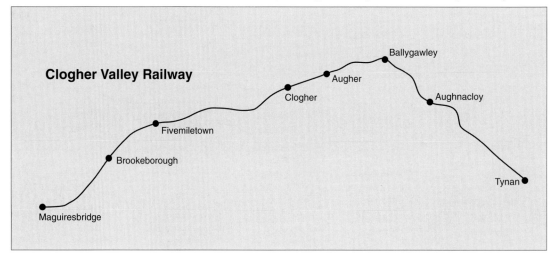

Clogher Valley Railway

(Map stations: Maguiresbridge, Brookeborough, Fivemiletown, Clogher, Augher, Ballygawley, Aughnacloy, Tynan)

CLOGHER VALLEY RAILWAY.

General Manager— WM. IRWIN, Esq., Aughnacloy.

DOWN.

DOWN	WEEK-DAYS					MARKET DAYS			
	a m	a.m.	pm	pm	pm	a m	a m	a m	pm
Tynan ..dep.	...	9 40	130	...	649	b	c	845	340
Caledon	a	9 44	134	...	654	...	...	850	345
Aughnacloy	653	1024	217	...	737	452	...	935	420
Ballygawley	715	1045	236	...	757	513	...	955	...
Augher	736	11 2	255	...	818	534	...	e	e
Clogher	746	1115	3 6	...	829	544	...	...	...
Fivemilet'wn	843	1145	343	525	9 1	626	645	...	...
Colebrooke ..	9 2	1159	4 0	542	...	645	7 3	...	...
Brookeboro'	914	12 8	411	553	...	657	716	...	...
Maguiresb'e	930	1220	427	6 5	...	713	730	...	...

UP.

UP	WEEK-DAYS					MARKET DAYS		
	a m	a.m.	pm	p m	pm	a.m.	a.m.	p m
Maguiresb'ed	...	9 54	157	4 45	615	7 50	d	...
Brookeboro' ..	...	10 3	215	4 58	632	8 7	...	...
Colebrooke ...	g	1016	227	5 7	644	8 21	...	...
Fivemiletown	520	1038	339	5 35	7 4	8 40	8 50	...
Clogher	6 1	1113	417	6 9	...	STOP	9 30	e
Augher	610	1124	427	6 19	...	c	9 38	...
Ballygawley ..	632	1145	448	6 39	...	...	9 58	2 0
Aughnacloy ..	714	1215	517	7 0	...	...	1016	2 27
Caledon	754	1256	6 0	...	...	...	...	...
Tynan ....arr.	759	1 0	6 5	...	...	...	...	3 16

a This train will not run on Enniskillen Fair Days (10th of each month). See Special Market Train **b**, and on Fivemiletown Fair Days will not leave Fivemiletown until 8-41 a.m. **b** Enniskillen Fair Days only. **c** Fivemiletown Fair days only. **d** Aughnacloy and Ballygawley Fair Days only. **e** Ballygawley Fair Days only. **g** On Enniskillen Fair Days this train will depart from Fivemiletown at 5-7 a.m.; Clogher arrive at 5-43 a.m.

status from tramway to railway but the locomotives, four Sharp Stewart 0-4-2Ts with enclosed motion and huge headlights fitted to the back of the cab — they always ran backwards — remained unchanged. As did the carriages, a fleet of American-style bogie clerestories entered from open end vestibules; a touch of modernity was steam heating. The Clogher Valley always struggled to make ends meet and in 1928 was taken over by Tyrone and Fermanagh County Councils. Improvements were made, chiefly in the form of a Walker Brothers diesel railcar, a pioneer vehicle to a

design later adopted by the County Donegal Railway. This took over most of the passenger workings and cut a whole hour from the schedule. However, not even the war could save the Clogher Valley and it closed on the first day of 1942.

The railcar passed to the County Donegal, and, as that company's No 10, is preserved at Cultra, along with *Phoenix*, which started out in 1928 as an experimental Atkinson-Walker steam tractor and was also sold to the County Donegal, which rebuilt it as a diesel.

Left:
Timetable for the period commencing August 1900.
Paul Collins collection

Above:
Aughnacloy, the headquarters of the Clogher Valley Railway. In this 1933 scene, nearest the camera are two of the original 0-4-2Ts built by Sharp Stewart in 1886/7. Beyond is the later No 7 *Blessingbourne*, a Hudswell Clarke 0-4-4T dating from 1910 and the company's newest steam locomotive. *LGRP*

Right:
The remains of one of the less fortunate 0-4-2Ts, No 4 *Fury*, at Aughnacloy, 1933.
Ian Allan Library

Top Left:
The Clogher Valley's weed-killing train, propelled by 0-4-2T No 2 *Errigal*, Aughnacloy, 1933. *LGRP*

Bottom Left:
Aughnacloy station, looking east. *LGRP*

Below:
No 6 *Erne* at Maguiresbridge. *LGRP*

Above:
Next but one station up the line from Aughnacloy was Ballygawley, four miles distant. Clogher Valley engines always ran cab first, hence the large headlight sported by 0-4-2T No 6 *Erne*, very necessary for a railway which ran for most of its length alongside, and some times right down the middle of, a main road. The passenger accommodation of *Erne's* mixed train is provided by one of the line's distinctive, open vestibule, clerestory-roofed, very transatlantic-looking bogie carriages. *Real Photos*

Top Left:
The handsome and substantial station at Clogher. A mixed train is heading east.
Real Photos

Bottom Left:
Fivemiletown station, with one of the company's 13 open vestibule carriages prominent.
Real Photos

Top Right:
Brookeborough station, looking west towards the end of the line at Maguiresbridge, 3½ miles distant, where a connection was made with the GNR Clones to Enniskillen line. *Real Photos*

Centre Right:
Much the most modern-looking and powerful Clogher Valley steam engine was No 4. Built by Hudswell Clarke in 1904, this 2-6-2T was bought by the Clogher Valley in 1936 from the Castlederg & Victoria Bridge Railway and is seen here after rebuilding. *LPC*

Bottom Right:
In a last-ditch attempt to keep the railway in business, the Clogher Valley was taken over by a joint committee appointed by Tyrone and Fermanagh County Councils in 1928. A Walker diesel railcar and a diesel tractor were bought; the railcar is seen here at Tynan, the eastern extremity of the line where it met the GNR's Armagh to Clones branch. However, not even the outbreak of World War 2 could save the Clogher Valley and its last train ran in the early hours of 1 January 1942.
Real Photos

4. Giant's Causeway Tramway

Built to connect Portrush, Northern Ireland's most popular tourist resort, with the Giant's Causeway, its most spectacular natural phenomenon, the Giant's Causeway, Portrush & Bush Valley Tramway and Railway opened in January 1883. A distinguished enterprise in a number of respects, it was the first hydro-electric powered line in the world. The power station was at Bushmills, six miles from Portrush. There were initial problems, so steam power had to be used for the first few months.

Electricity was taken from a third rail (on its opening day the Engineer removed his trousers and sat on the live rail to prove how safe it was), but this was changed to overhead in 1899, after which electric trams were the normal method of transport, although steam-hauled extras were provided for a while at peak holiday periods. Goods traffic lasted for some 10 years but had disappeared by the late 1890s, which was probably a relief to the operators, as they were able to rebuild the goods wagons as passenger trailers and thus cope better with the huge demand during the holiday season. Five GEC-built motor cars provided the accommodation, assisted by 11 open and four closed four-wheel trailers. In later years the Tramway closed down for the winter, and in the end this long annual lay-off was not compensated for by the four busy summer

---

GIANT'S CAUSEWAY AND PORTRUSH ELECTRIC TRAMWAY.

W. A. TRAILL, Esq., C.E., Engineer. D. FALL, Esq., Secretary and Manager.

PORTRUSH Departure.		CAUSEWAY Departure.	BUSHMILLS Departure.		
			8-10 a.m. Train leaves P'rush at	9- 0 am B'fast Ex.	
9- 5 am on arr. of train at 9- 0 am		9-30 a.m.	9-45 a.m.	9-30 ,, for Derry	
10-40 ,, ,, 10-35 ,,		10-10 ,,	10-25 ,,	11-15 ,, ,, B'fast	
11-15 ,, ,, 11-10 ,,				11-50 ,, ,, Derry	
12-55 p m ,, 12-50 pm		12-15 p.m.	12-30 p.m. ,,	12-10 pm ,, B'fast	
c 1-25 ,, ,, 1-20 ,, Derry		1-45 ,,	2- 0 ,, ,,	2- 0 ,, ,, Derry	
1-45 ,, (Satur. only) 1-40 ,, B'fast				3-15 ,, Bft—Lrne	
2-30 ,, on arr. of train at 2-20 ,, DCR		3-45 ,,	4- 0 ,, ,,	3-50 ,, for B'fast	
3-10 ,, ,, 3- 5 ,, B'fast		4-45 ,,	5- 0 ,, ,,	5- 5 ,, ,, Derry	
4-55 ,, ,, 4-45 ,, Derry				6-20 ,, B'fast Ex,	
5-55 ,, ,, 5-50 ,, B'fast		6-10 ,,	6-25 ,, ,,	6-25 ,, for B'fast	
7-30 ,, ,, 6-10 ,, C'rne		7-10 ,,	7-25 ,, ,,	7-30 ,, ,, Derry	
7-30 ,, B'fast				8- 0 ,, Bft Ex, Sat	
				10- 0 ,, Coleraine	

c Satur. excepted.

SUNDAY SERVICE.

9- 5 a.m. on arr. of train	[& Derry		10- 0 a.m. Train leav. P'rush		
at 9- 0 a.m. f'm B'fast				at 10-45 a.m. Col'raine	
11- 5 ,, 10-15 ,, ,, C'town			11- 5 ,,	1-45 p.m. ,,	
,, 11- 0 ,, ,, Belfast		10-50 a.m.			
11-35 ,, ,, 11-30 ,, ,,		1-30 p.m.	1-45 p.m.		
12-25 p.m. ,, 12-20 p.m. ,, Derry		2-15 ,,	2-30 ,, ,,	3-35 ,, Bft & D'ry	
3- 0 ,, ,, 2-50 ,, ,, Coler'ie		4-45 ,,	5- 0 ,, ,,	6- 0 ,, Cookst'wn	
3-30 ,,				6-45 ,, Belfast	
6- 0 ,,		5-45 ,,	6- 0 ,, ,,	7-10 ,, Derry	

NOTE.—This Time Table is subject to alterations without notice.
The Company will not hold themselves responsible for the running of the Tramcars at the hours stated, nor for delays which may occur upon the road.

FARES—				
Portrush and Bushmills........8d;	*Return, 1s 0d.	First Class, 1s 0d.	*Return, 1s 6d	
Portrush and Giant's Causeway 1s.	,, 1s 6d.	,, 1s 6d.	,, 2s 0d	
Portrush and Dunluce..........6d.	,, 10d.	,, 8d.		
Portrush and Giant's Head......4d.		,, 5d.		
Short Journey Tickets.........3d.		,, 6d.		

months, the line closing completely in 1949. Much regret was expressed at the time, but eventually its demise came to be accepted as inevitable and permanent. However, in what we might consider the more enlightened 1990s, the Giant's Causeway & Bushmills Railway is being revived, finance has been secured for its reopening (nearly half a million pounds from the Northern Ireland Tourist Board), the track is being relaid as I write, and soon a narrow gauge steam-operated railway will be once more be conveying jolly holidaymakers along the Antrim Coast between Bushmills and the Causeway.

Left:
Timetable for the period commencing August 1900. *Paul Collins collection*

Above:
The Giant's Causeway terminus of the Giant's Causeway Tramway. An open electric car is on the left, a closed one with two open-sided trailers is berthed on the right. *H. C. Casserley*

Right:
Interior view of Giant's Causeway carriage No 2. After closure in 1949 this became a garden shed but was rescued by the Museum in the late 1960s, restored and mounted on County Donegal wheels. *Author*

5. Castlederg & Victoria Bridge Tramway

This seven-mile-long County Tyrone tramway ran from the GNR's Belfast to Derry main line at Victoria Bridge through the intermediate stations at Fyfin, Crew and Spamount to Castlederg. Opened in April 1883, over the years it owned six locomotives, but never more than three at any one time. The three original Kitson tramway type 0-4-0Ts had all gone by 1912. At the end in 1933 there was a Hudswell Clarke 2-6-0T, which was sold to the Clogher Valley Railway, an 0-4-4T from the same maker and a Beyer Peacock Isle of Man type 2-4-0T which had originated on the Ballymena &

Larne. The journey took 40min. All trains were mixed; there were normally four a day in each direction, although on occasions extras were run. There were no passing loops. There were seven end-vestibuled carriages and 29 wagons.

The Tramway had a roadside location throughout its length and for much of its existence was well patronised and prosperous, but the usual scenario of increasing motor competition brought about its end during the 1933 railway strike. The sole surviving relic is carriage No 4 at Cultra.

CASTLEDERG AND VICTORIA BRIDGE TRAMWAY.

W. J. DAVIDSON, *Secretary and Manager.*

Miles.	DOWN.	WEEK-DAYS.								Miles.	UP.	WEEK-DAYS.							
		a.m.	a.m.	a.m.	p.m.	p.m.	p.m.					a.m.	a.m.	a.m.	p.m.	p.m.	p.m.		
	Castlederg....	7 15	8*15	1035	12†30	1 30	3 40	....			Vict'ria Bridge	8 5	9 b5	1155	2†15	2 45	5 35	....
1½	Spamount....	Fris. & Sat.	8 23	1043	....	1 38	3 48	....	2	Fyfin	Fris. & Sat.	9 22	1212	....	3 2	5 52	....
3	Crew		8 31	1051	....	1 46	3 56	....	3½	Crew		9 29	1219	....	3 9	5 59	....
5	Fyfin		8 38	1058	....	1 53	4 3	....	5½	Spamount....		9 37	1227	....	3 17	6 7	....
7	Vict'ria Bridge	7 55	8 55	1115	1 10	2 10	4 20	....	7	Castlederg....	8 40	9 45	1235	2 55	3 25	6 15	....

* On Fridays this train *will not* leave Castlederg till 8-42 a.m., and *will not* stop at intermediate stations, and will not run on Sats. † Castlederg Fair Days only. b On Sats. this train will not run.

Above:
Timetable for the period commencing August 1900.
Paul Collins collection

Left:
The Castlederg terminus of the Castlederg & Victoria Bridge Tramway.
Ian Allan Library

Right:
Timetable for the period commencing August 1900.
Paul Collins collection

6. Ballymena & Larne Railway

Opened for goods in July 1877, the BLR began regular passenger services, the first on the Irish narrow gauge, in August 1878. The line ran for 32 miles from Ballymena, where it was extended in 1880 to the broad gauge (5ft 3in) station, to the port of Larne. It shared a station there with the broad gauge BNCR.

The BLR was taken over by the BNCR in July 1889. The timetable consisted of four trains a day in each direction, those that stopped at all stations taking 1¾ hr.

The Ballymena & Larne is chiefly remembered for its boat trains of the interwar years. These, covering the distance in one hour, were the fastest narrow gauge trains in Ireland and the most comfortable, being provided in 1928 with handsome corridor carriages fitted with lavatories and electric lighting, which were in all respects comparable with those being built by the LMS for its main line expresses on both sides of the Irish Sea. Hauled by 4-4-2Ts transferred from the Ballycastle Railway and fitted with cut-down cabs and boiler mountings, which enhanced their air of purposefulness and power, they represented the high point of steam on the narrow gauge. Sadly they were unable to halt the drain of traffic to the roads and passenger services ended in 1933, although the section of line between Ballyclare Paper Mills and Larne Harbour remained open until July 1950.

BELFAST AND NORTHERN COUNTIES RAILWAY. [AUG, 1900'

BALLYMENA AND LARNE BRANCH.

Single. 1 cl. s d	Single. 3 cl. s d	Return. 1 cl. s d	Return. 3 cl. s d	Miles.	DOWN TRAINS.	Week-days a.m.	Week-days a.m.	Week-days a.m.	Week-days a.m.	Week-days a.m.	Week-days p m	Week-days p m	Week-days	Sundays a.m.	Sundays a.m.	Sundays p.m.	Sundays p.m.
							Mail.	Saturdays only.	Third Wed. of month.								
					LARNE HARBOUR ..dep.	b	**7 56**		....	b	**1 55**	**6 0**	....	....	....	**5 5**	**6 30**
0 2	0 1	0 3	0 2	1	Larne	6 35			8 40	10 0	2 0	6 5	....	**7 35**	....	5 10	6 35
0 10	0 6	1 3	0 9	6¼	Headwood	a			a	....	a	a	....	a	....	a	a
1 0	0 7	1 6	0 11	7¾	Ballyboley ......arr.	6 55			9 5	1030	2 20	6 30	....	7 55	....	5 29	6 55
....	....	....	....	....	Branch. Ballyboley .....dep.	7 10			9 10	1040	2 25	6 40	....	8 0	....	5 30	6 56
1 2	0 8	1 9	1 0	9½	Branch. Ballynure	7 15	....		9 18	1048	2 33	6 48	....	8 6	....	5 36	7 2
1 6	0 10	2 3	1 3	11½	Branch. Ballyclare	7 20	....		9 26	1056	2 40	6 56	....	8 12	....	5 42	7 8
1 7	0 11	2 4	1 4	13½	Branch. Doagh ......arr.	7 30	....		9 35	11 5	2 50	7 5	....	8 18	....	5 48	7 14
....	....	....	....	....	Branch. Doagh ....dep.	6 35	....	8 0		1010	1 45	6 10	....	7 30	1015	....	6 30
....	....	....	....	....	Branch. Ballyclare	6 43	....	8 5		1018	1 53	6 18	....	7 36	1021	....	6 36
....	....	....	....	....	Branch. Ballynure	6 50	....	8 10		1025	2 0	6 27	....	7 42	1027	....	6 42
....	....	....	....	....	Branch. Ballyboley ....arr.	6 55	....	8 15		1030	2 8	6 35	....	7 50	1033	....	6 48
1 6	0 11	2 3	1 4	12	Ballynashee ....dep.	7 20	....	8 35		11 0	2 40	6 53	....	8 13	1051	....	7 13
2 2	1 3	3 3	1 10	17½	Moorfields	7 35	....	8 50		1118	2 53	7 8	....	8 29	11 7	....	7 29
2 6	1 5	3 9	2 2	20½	Kells	7 43	....	8 58		1128	3 3	7 18	....	8 38	1116	....	7 38
3 0	1 8	4 6	2 6	25¼	**BALLYMENA** ......arr.	**8 0**	**8 56**	**9 10**		**1150**	**3 15**	**7 40**	....	8 50	1128	....	**7 50**

Single. 1 cl. s d	Single. 3 cl. s d	Return. 1 cl. s d	Return. 3 cl. s d	Miles.	UP TRAINS.	Week-days e a.m.	Week-days a.m.	Week-days a.m.	Week-days a.m.	Week-days p m	Week-days p m	Week-days p m	Week-days	Sundays a.m.	Sundays p.m.	Sundays p.m.	Sundays
							3rd Class only.	2nd Thur. of month & Larne ½ yearly fairdays			Mail.						
					BALLYMENA ......dep.	**6b15**			**9 45**	**1b20**	**4 40**	**5b35**	....	**9 0**	**2 0**	**8 15**	....
0 7	0 4	0 11	0 6	4¼	Kells	6 30			10 0	1 40		5 57	....	9 12	2 12	8 27	....
0 11	0 6	1 4	0 9	7¼	Moorfields	6 38			10 8	1 48		6 6	....	9 21	2 21	8 36	....
1 7	0 11	2 6	1 5	12¾	Ballynashee	6 55			1020	2 5		6 23	....	9 37	2 37	8 52	....
2 0	1 2	3 0	1 9	17	Ballyboley	7 5			1030	2 25		6 41	....	9 55	2 55	9 10	....
....	....	....	....	....	Branch Ballyboley ....dep.	....			1040	2 25		6 40	....	9 55	....	9 10	....
2 3	1 4	3 4	2 0	18¾	Branch Ballynure	....			1048	2 33		6 48	....	10 1	....	9 16	....
2 6	1 5	3 9	2 2	20¾	Branch Ballyclare	....			1056	2 40	....	6 56	....	10 7	....	9 22	....
2 8	1 6	4 0	2 3	23	Branch Doagh ....arr.	....			11 5	2 50	....	7 5	....	1013	....	9 28	....
....	....	....	....	....	Branch Doagh ....dep.	....	6 35	8b30	1010	1 45	....	6 10	....	9 25	....	8 40	....
....	....	....	....	....	Branch Ballyclare	....	6 43	8 38	1018	1 53	....	6 18	....	9 31	....	8 46	....
....	....	....	....	....	Branch Ballynure	....	6 50	8 45	1025	2 0	....	6 27	....	9 37	....	8 52	....
....	....	....	....	....	Branch Ballyboley	....	6 55	8 50	1030	2 8	....	6 35	....	9 43	....	8 58	....
2 4	1 4	3 6	2 0	18½	Headwood	a	....	a	a	a	....	....	....	a	a	a	....
2 10	1 7	4 3	2 5	23¾	Larne	7 45	7 45	9 30	1055	2 45	....	7 5	....	1015	3 15	9 30	....
3 0	1 8	4 6	2 6	25¼	**LARNE HARBOUR**...arr.	....	....	....	**11 0**	**2 50**	**5 40**	**7 10**	....	**1020**	**3 20**	....	....

All trains 1st and 3rd class. *b* The above trains convey goods and passengers and cannot observe any stated tim

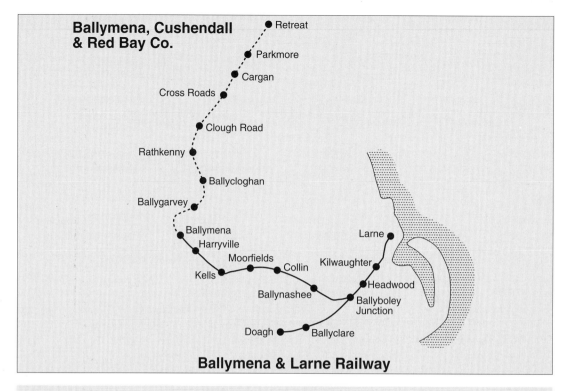

Ballymena, Cushendall & Red Bay Co.

- Retreat
- Parkmore
- Cargan
- Cross Roads
- Clough Road
- Rathkenny
- Ballycloghan
- Ballygarvey
- Ballymena
- Harryville
- Moorfields
- Kells
- Collin
- Ballynashee
- Doagh
- Ballyclare
- Larne
- Kilwaughter
- Headwood
- Ballyboley Junction

Ballymena & Larne Railway

Below:

No 105, one of the original Ballymena & Larne Beyer Peacock 2-4-0Ts of 1877. Initially No 2, it was renumbered by the Belfast & Northern Counties Railway in 1897 but is otherwise in original typical Beyer Peacock condition. One can see the resemblance to the similar locomotives built for, and still working at, the Isle of Man. No 105 was broken up in 1933. *LPC*

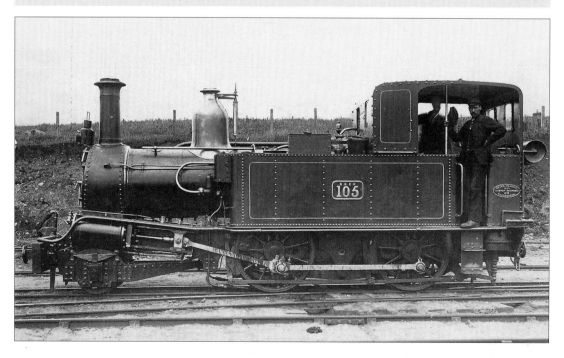

Above:
No 109, originally No 5. This, another Beyer Peacock design, is a 2-6-0ST dating from 1880. It was broken up in 1934. *LPC*

Below:
No 106, a Beyer Peacock 0-6-0T of 1877, originally No 3, comes bustling into Larne Town with a short train from Ballymena some time in the 1920s. Note the broad gauge track on either side of No 106. This locomotive was scrapped in 1933. *LGRP*

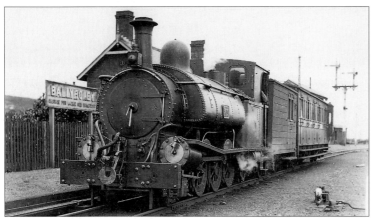

Above:
Larne Town shed and workshops in 1936. *LGRP*

Centre Left:
A goods brake van, a 6-ton box van and an open wagon at Larne at the time of closure in 1950. *LGRP*

Bottom Left:
A train for Doagh at Ballyboley, 9 August 1930, shortly before passenger traffic on the branch ceased. The rather transatlantic-looking locomotive is Beyer Peacock 2-6-0ST No 109 of 1880. It was scrapped in 1934, the year after the branch closed down completely. *H. C. Casserley*

Top Right
Doagh with No 109 about to set off back to Ballyboley, 9 August 1930. *H. C. Casserley*

Right:
No 106 and baskets of coal, Ballymena, 1931. *LGRP*

7. Ballymena, Cushendall & Red Bay Co.

Essentially a mineral railway, this line opened in May 1875 and was actually the very first Irish narrow gauge railway to be sanctioned by Parliament. It ran 17 miles from Ballymena to Retreat and for a while enjoyed considerable prosperity, serving the iron mines in the district, which were connected to the main line by sidings and branches, some of which were owned by the mining companies. However, the market collapsed, traffic followed suit, and in 1884 the Belfast & Northern Counties took over. Two years later the first passenger trains were introduced. These terminated at Parkmore, 3¾ miles from Retreat.

For most of the 17 miles northeast from Ballymena, trains struggled against the grade, the summit at Essathohan siding being, at 1,045ft above sea level, the highest point reached by an Irish railway. The usual pattern of four trains in each direction was followed, the northbound journey taking 50min, southbound 10min less. The tourist attractions of Cushendall and Glenariff were never reached by the railway, visitors having to hire road transport from the railhead.

Three Black Hawthorn 0-4-2STs provided the original motive power; these were replaced by the BNCR. Passengers were carried in tramway type bogie carriages. Passenger traffic ended in 1930, goods traffic in 1940.

Below:
Timetable for the period commencing August 1900. *Paul Collins collection*

BALLYMENA AND CUSHENDALL BRANCH.

DOWN TRAINS.	WEEK-DAYS.					UP TRAINS.	WEEK-DAYS.				
	a.m.	a.m.	p m	p m	Trains stop only on notice to Guard		a m	p.m.	p.m.	p m	a 3-45 pm. stops on notice to Guard
BALLYMENA ......dep.	7 35	9 50†	1 30	5 15		**PARKMORE** ......dep.	8 25	3 45	5 20	6 20	
*Ballygarvey	7 42	9 57	1 37	5 22		Cargan	8 30			6 25	
Ballcloughan	7 47	10 2	1 42	5 27		Cross Roads	8 35			6 30	
Rathkenny	7 52	10 7	1 47	5 32		Knockanally	8 42	4 3		6 38	
Clough Road	7 56	10 11		5 36		Clough Road	8 50			6 42	
Knockanally	8 2	10 17	1 58	5 42		Rathkenny	8 53	a		6 46	
Cross Roads	8 10	10 25	2 6	5 50		Ballcloughan	8 58	a		6 50	
Cargan	8 16	10 31	2 13	5 56		*Ballygarvey	9 3			6 55	
PARKMORE ......arr.	8 22	10 37	2 20	6 2		**BALLYMENA** ......arr.	9 10	4 25	6 5	7 5	

† On Mondays, Wednesdays, and Saturdays the 9-50 am train will wait until 10-20 am and connect with 9-15 am from Belfast during August, and Mondays and Saturdays during September.

FARES FOR THE SINGLE JOURNEY.

	S. D.	S. D.
Between Ballymena and Ballycloughan or Ballygarvey	0 6	0 3
Between Ballymena and Rathkenny, Clough Road, or Knockanally	0 9	0 6
Between Ballymena and Cargan or Parkmore	1 6	1 0
Between Ballycloughan and Rathkenny, Clough Road, or Knockanally	0 6	0 3
Between Cross Roads and Knockanally, Cargan, or Parkmore	0 6	0 3

8. Ballycastle Railway

Opened in October 1880, this line ran 17 miles from Ballymoney, on the B&NCR's main line to Londonderry, to the Antrim coastal resort of Ballycastle. It never made much money and actually closed down for a period in 1924 until rescued by its backer, the NCC, which took it over completely.

The service consisted in the main of three return journeys a day. These took between 50min and one hour. The best was a summer Saturday nonstop run accomplished in 40min. Initially motive power was provided by three Black Hawthorn 0-6-0STs, unusual motive power for an Irish narrow gauge railway; two powerful Kitson 4-4-2Ts arrived in 1908. Carriages were initially compartment type, painted two shades of brown; these were largely displaced by LMS-designed corridor stock transferred from the Ballymena & Larne in 1933. The Ballycastle Railway closed in July 1950.

Right:
Ballycastle Railway Beyer Peacock 2-4-2T No 110 of 1892 in original condition. It was later rebuilt as a 2-4-4T.
LPC

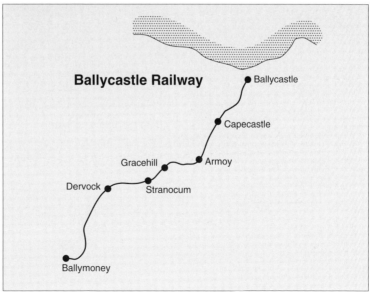

Above:
Bowman Malcolm was locomotive superintendent of the Belfast & Northern Counties Railway for the remarkable span of 46 years, from 1876 to 1922. For a period he was much addicted to the Worsdell von Borries system of compounding for both his broad and narrow gauge locomotives. No 43, seen here at Ballymoney shed in 1948, was one such compound, a 2-4-2T built at Derby as late as 1920. *LGRP*

Below:
Former Ballymena & Larne 0-6-0T No 106 at Ballymoney, in charge of one of the bogie corridor carriages, miniature versions of contemporary broad gauge express stock, built by the LMS in 1926 for the Ballymena-Larne boat trains and transferred when passenger traffic ceased on that line in 1933. This picture must have been taken in that latter year, for that was when No 106 was taken out of traffic. *LPC*

Above
A view of Ballycastle station in 1931. *LGRP*

Right:
No 3, one of two impressive-looking 4-4-2Ts built by Kitsons in 1908 for the Ballycastle Railway. They were renumbered and eventually transferred to the Larne line in 1930, which entailed the cutting down of their cabs and boiler fittings, which rather added to their sense of purposefulness. Seen here as built. *LPC*

Below Right:
NCC 4-4-2T No 114, formerly Ballycastle No 4, in its altered form as working on the Larne line in 1940. *LPC*

Above:
The last weekend of the Ballycastle line, 3 July 1950. 2-4-2T No 41 approaches Ballymoney. *Ian Allan Library*

Left:
Between 1900 and 1960 the British Aluminium Co operated a 4-mile narrow gauge line to carry ore from its factory at Larne to the harbour and it was connected to the Ballymena & Larne Railway. One of its locomotives, No 2, a Peckett 0-4-0T of 1906, was sold to George Cohen in 1955 and was used in the lifting of the Ballycastle line before being donated to the Belfast Railway Museum, where it is seen here. *Author*

9. Bessbrook & Newry Tramway

Like the original Giant's Causeway, this was a hydro-electric powered line. It was opened in September 1895 to link Newry with the mills at Bessbrook, three miles distant. Current was fed through a third rail, except at the level crossing at Millvale where overhead was provided. Trams ran every hour, the journey taking 20min. The line closed in January 1948. The trackbed is best seen from the Craigmore Viaduct on the Dublin to Belfast main line.

Below
Bessbrook & Newry tramcar No 1, built by Hurst Nelson in 1921, at Bessbrook, 4 June 1932. This was the company's most up-to-date vehicle. It was 37ft 1¾in long and seated 40 passengers.
H. C. Casserley

BESSBROOK AND NEWRY ELECTRIC RAILWAY.

J. L. D. MEARES, Esq., C.E., *Engineer.*   J. DAWSON, *General Manager.*   W. SCOTT, *Secretary.*

† Except Sats.	WEEK-DAYS.												SATS. ONLY.				SUN	
	a.m.	a.m.	a.m.	a.m.	p.m.	p.m.	p.m.	p.m.	p.m.	p.m.	p.m.	p.m.†	p.m.†	p.m.	p.m.	p.m.	a.m.	p.m.
Bessbrook ....dep.	8 30	9 27	1025	1130	1230	1 30	2 25	3 25	4 30	5 25	6 10	7 35	6 30	7 35	8 30	9 23	10 5	1 5
Newry ....arr.	8 50	9 47	1045	1150	1250	1 50	2 45	3 45	4 50	5 45	6 50	7 55	6 50	7 55	8 50	9 40	1025	1 25
Newry ....dep.	9 0	9 55	1055	1155	1 0	1 55	2 55	4 0	4 55	5 50	7† 5	8†15	7 10	8 5	8 55	9 40	1030	1 30
Bessbrook ....arr.	9 25	1023	1125	1225	1 28	2 22	3 22	4 28	5 25	6 25	7 30	8 40	7 35	8 28	9 22	10 5	1055	1 55

All Trains stop at Mullaghglass and Derramore, Millvale or Craigmore, when required.

Above:
Timetable for the period commencing August 1900.
Paul Collins collection

Below:
Bessbrook & Newry car No 2. Originally built in 1885 for the opening of the line, a new body was grafted on in 1942. Well, hardly new. It came from a former Dublin & Lucan tram which had once been steam-hauled but was converted to electric propulsion in 1899. This body was a bit too short for its new underframe, so a luggage compartment was added and in this form it ran until the line closed down on 10 January 1948. However, No 2's career was far from over, for it was returned whence it had come, Ashbury's of Manchester 63 years earlier, and served as a cricket pavilion. It was given to the Belfast Transport Museum in 1955, sailed back across the Irish Sea, and was restored by the museum staff. It is seen at Cultra in December 1998. *Author*

10. Cavan & Leitrim Railway

The Cavan & Leitrim was unique in Ireland in that in its later years coal was the chief reason for its continuing existence. A public meeting held at Ballinamore in September 1883 declared that a light railway and tramway would 'open up the coal and iron districts of Arigna and Lough Allen'. It is now another line that is experiencing a revival.

Opened for goods on 17 October 1887 and for passengers on 24 October, the Cavan & Leitrim ran from Belturbet, in County Cavan, to Dromod in County Leitrim. This section was a light railway. A tramway ran from Ballinamore, roughly halfway between the two termini, to Arigna, close to the shores of Lough Allen.

Both lines were operated from the outset by a fleet of eight 4-4-0Ts built by Robert Stephenson & Co. Latterly locomotives from other narrow gauge lines absorbed by the GSR and CIE appeared. The four 2-4-2Ts from the Cork,

Blackrock & Passage section were transferred by the GSR when that line was closed in 1932, and between 1941 and 1957 four Tralee & Dingle engines, three 2-6-0Ts and one 2-6-2T, were sent to the Cavan & Leitrim. The carriages were distinctive-looking bogie vehicles with clerestory roofs, with seating arranged along the sides, verandas at the ends. Two Tralee & Dingle carriages were transferred there in 1954. There were six four-wheel passenger brake vans and the usual assortment of freight vehicles.

Ballinamore was the hub of the line; the locomotive depot and works were there,

Below:
Timetable for the period commencing August 1900. *Paul Collins collection*

CAVAN AND LEITRIM RAILWAY COMPANY, LTD.

Traffic Manager—W. H. M'Adoo, Esq., Ballinamore.

DOWN.		a.m.	a.m.	a.m.	p m	p m	UP.		a.m.	p m	p m	p m	
BELTURBET ....dep.			8 15		1 0	6 30	**DROMOD** ....dep.		7 35	1 0	5 40		
Tomkin Road......(b) ,,			8 27		1 12	6 42	Dereen ....(b) ,,		7 45	1 10	5 50		
Ballyconnell .... ,,			8 43		1 29	6 58	Mohill .... ,,		8 0	1 32	6 6		
Ballyheady ....(b) ,,			8 50		1 36	7 5	Rosharry .... ,,		8b 5	1a37	6 11		
Bawnboy Road....... ,,			9 3		1 47	7 15	Adoon ....(b) ,,		8 14	1 46	6 20		
Killyran ....(b) ,,			9 9		1 53	7 21	Fenagh.............(b) ,,		8 22	1 54	6 28		
Garadice............. ,,			9 14		1 58	7 26	Lawderdale.........(b) ,,		8 26	1 58	6 32		
Ballinamore ....arr.			9 26		2 10	7 38	Ballinamore..........arr.		8 31	2 3	6 37		
(Drumshambo Line.) Ballinamore....dep.			10 0		2 35	7 50	*(Drumshambo Line.)* Arigna ....dep.		7 10	12 20	4 40		
Ballyduff .... ,,			10 15		2 50	8 5	Drumshambo ... ,,		7 27	12 46	4 58		
Cornabrone....(b) ,,			10 32		3 7	8 22	Creagh ....(b) ,,		7 37	12 56	5 8		
Annadale.....(b) ,,			10 42		3 17	8 32	Kiltubrid ...... ,,		7 48	1 7	5 19		
Kiltubrid ..... ,,			10 49		3 24	8 39	Annadale.....(b) ,,		7 54	1 13	5 25		
Creagh ....(b) ,,			10 59		3 34	8 49	Cornabrone....(b) ,,		8 4	1 23	5 35		
Drumshambo ... ,,			11 11		3 50	8 59	Ballyduff .... ,,		8 22	1 41	5 53		
Arigna ....arr.			11 27		4 6		Ballinamore ....arr.		8 36	1 55	6 7		
Ballinamore.........dep.			9 45		2 17	7 48	Ballinamore..........dep.		8 36	2 25	6 45		
Lawderdale.........(b) ,,			9 50		2 23	7 53	Garadice.............. ,,		8 43	2 37	6 57		
Fenagh.............(b) ,,			9 54		2 27	7 57	Killyran ....(b) ,,		8 53	2 42	7 2		
Adoon ....(b) ,,			10 2		2 35	8 5	Bawnboy Road....... ,,		9 0	2 52	7 12		
Rosharry .... ,,			10a11		2 44	8b14	Ballyheady ....(b) ,,		9 6	2 58	7 18		
Mohill.............. ,,			10 24		2 53	8 23	Ballyconnell .... ,,		9 16	3 12	7 30		
Dereen ....(b) ,,			10 36		3 5	8 35	Tomkin Road........(b) ,,		9 26	3 22	7 40		
DROMOD ....arr.			10 46		3 15	8 45	**BELTURBET** ....arr.		9 38	3 34	7 52		

a Stops by Signal   b Stops by Signal on Tuesdays and Thursdays only.

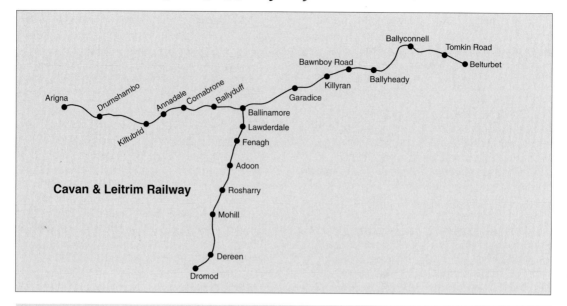

Cavan & Leitrim Railway

Below:
Cavan & Leitrim 4-4-0T No 2 *Kathleen* at Ballinamore in 1934. Built by Robert Stephenson in 1887, this was one of eight identical locomotives built for the line's opening. *Real Photos*

although after the 1925 amalgamation heavy overhauls were carried out at Inchicore. At Belturbet the line connected with the Great Northern Railway's broad gauge branch to Ballyhaise on the Clones to Cavan branch, and at Dromod with the Midland & Great Western Railway's main line from Dublin to Sligo. In 1920 the line was finally extended up the Arigna Valley to the mines located there.

At its maximum the timetable showed three mixed trains each way on all three routes out of Ballinamore. In the Cavan & Leitrim's final years there were three return trains between Ballinamore and Dromod and one each way to Belturbet and to Arigna.

The Cavan & Leitrim was unique in that it used native coal, mined at Arigna. Although this burned much more quickly than the imported product, its proximity made it cheaper.

By the 1930s the Cavan & Leitrim was in deep trouble, suffering badly from road competition. One economy measure was the demolition of the carriage sheds, which led to

the condition of the carriages 'gradually becoming appalling,' to quote Patrick J. Flanagan, the line's historian.

The Cavan & Leitrim survived World War 2 but the opening of a power station on the shores of Lough Allen, which would take all the coal the Arigna mines could produce and would not need the services of the railway, was the final nail in its coffin. There had been talk of dieselisation but it never happened and the line closed on 31 March 1959, the last exclusively steam-worked narrow gauge line in Ireland.

Various bits and pieces remain. Engine No 3 *Lady Edith* was shipped to America and No 2 *Kathleen* lives in the Railway Museum at Cultra. I found myself travelling in an open carriage mounted on a Cavan & Leitrim underframe at Stradbally in 1980. A new C&L Railway Company has been set up in the 1990s to revive part of the line. Based at the restored Dromod terminus, track has been relaid to the first level crossing at Cloncarry and train rides, with steam and diesel traction, are available.

Below:
A Cavan & Leitrim 4-4-0T entering Drumshambo station. *Author's collection*

Above:
A pair of Cavan & Leitrim 4-4-0Ts at Ballinamore, 2 April 1956. On the left is No 4 formerly *Violet* with the 12.20pm Dromod to Belturbet; on the right No 3 *Lady Edith* shunts cattle wagons. *W. A. C. Smith*

Below:
No 3 *Lady Edith* approaches Ballinamore from Arigna with a goods train. It is Ballinamore Fair Day and the vans will be needed to take cattle to Mohill and Ballyconnell later in the afternoon; 3 September 1957. *R. K. Walton*

Above:
The Cavan & Leitrim was the last entirely steam-worked public narrow gauge railway in Ireland and as such it acquired locomotives from other lines as they closed down. Former Tralee & Dingle 2-6-0T No 3, a Hunslet engine of 1889 transferred in 1941, is on an Arigna branch train in the 1950s.
P. B. Whitehouse

Below:
Four 2-4-2Ts built for the Cork, Blackrock & Passage Railway by Neilsons in 1900 were transferred to the Cavan & Leitrim in 1934. No 12, which had called itself No 6 when living down south, is seen at Ballyconnell with the 12.45 Dromod to Belturbet on 11 September 1948. *I. L. Wright*

Top Left:
Mohill, looking towards
Belturbet in 1939. *LGRP*

Bottom Left:
The ropeway connecting the
railway with the Arigna coal
mines, at the transfer point
where coal was loaded into
railway wagons.
Real Photos

Top Right:
Two of the original Cavan &
Leitrim engines survived the
closure of 31 March 1959. No 3
Lady Edith is seen here at
Allaire Park Station, New
Jersey, USA, in May 1967
with some Tralee & Dingle
vehicles beyond.
Edgar T. Mead

Centre Right:
No 2 *Kathleen* has been
preserved much nearer home
at the museum at Cultra.
Author

Below:
The narrow gauge itself is
making a comeback at
Dromod and a carriage body
is seen here in August 1993.
The Irish Rail signalbox on the
Dublin–Sligo line is seen on
the far left. *Author*

11. West Clare & South Clare Railways

The West Clare opened from Ennis, alongside the Waterford, Limerick & Western Railway's broad gauge station, to Milltown Malbay, 27 miles distant on the Atlantic coast, in July 1887. The South Clare was an extension to Moyasta Junction, 16 miles to the south, where one line headed south for four miles to Kilrush on the Shannon, the other to the small coastal resort of Kilkee, five miles distant, a place with 'an excellent golf course and very bracing air,' to quote Hugh Fayle. A less than properly cooked shellfish there poisoned much of my family, or so the mother-in-law claims, but that is another story. The South Clare opened in August 1892 for goods and four months later for passengers.

From the outset the entire network was operated by the West Clare Railway. Notorious (and ridiculed — it lost a libel action against a poet who lampooned it) for its inefficiency and especially for the lateness of its trains, and unpopular with local farmers who claimed its trains regularly murdered their livestock which just happened to be grazing on its tracks, the West Clare got a grip on itself in the first decade of the present century, invested in much more powerful motive power, and became quite virtuous.

Its first engines were four Bagnall 0-6-0Ts, which were severely underpowered and disappeared around the turn of the century. Much more suitable were three Dübs 0-6-2Ts of 1892, followed by three 2-6-2Ts, one from Dübs, two from the Leeds firm of Thomas Green & Son. A quirk of the 0-6-2Ts was that all eight wheels were of the same diameter. Five 4-6-0Ts, from Kerr Stuart, Bagnall and Hunslet, completed the West Clare's fleet, the first arriving in 1903, the last two in 1922, these being the very last steam engines built for the narrow gauge in Ireland, other than for Bord na Móna. There were originally 35 six-wheel carriages, many of them narrow gauge versions of broad gauge compartment stock, but there were also some curious-looking clerestory-roofed saloons.

Although holiday traffic in summer helped balance the books, the bread and butter (the latter rather thinly spread) business was serving the local community. In Great Southern days buses, cars and lorries ate steadily into

---

Secretary—W. J. KENNEDY, 39 Dame Street, Dublin.] WEST CLARE RAILWAY. [Manager—P. SULLIVAN, Ennis

DOWN

FARES 1cl (s d)	3cl (s d)	Miles	1st & 3rd class.	a m	a m	p m	p m	p m	SUN p m
			ENNIS ......dep.	5 0	8 20	12 5	3 15	7 0	5 0
		8¾	Corofin	5 25	8 45	1230	340	725	5 25
1 9	1 0	12	Willbrook	...	flag	...	fl'g	...	...
2 0	1 4	18½	Ennistymon	6 5	9 25	1 5	415	8 0	6 5
3 8	2 1	20¾	Lehinch	615	9 40	1 15	425	810	6 15
4 0	2 3	27	Milltown Malbay	640	10 5	1 35	445	835	6 40
5 0	3 0	31¼	Quilty	655	1020	flag	...	850	6 55
5 9	3 5	32½	Kilmurry	7 0	1025	flag	5 5	855	7 0
6 2	3 8	34½	Craggaknock	fl'g	flag	flag	...	fl'g	flag
6 0	4 0	37¾	Doonbeg	720	1045	2 15	535	915	7 20
7 2	4 3	43	Moyasta Junc. a.	740	1120	2 35	555	945	7 40
...	...	45¼	Blackweir	750	flag	flag	...	fl'g	7 50
...	...	47	Kilrush	8 0	1135	2 50	610	100	8 0
...	...	48	kilkee	8 0	135	2 50	...	100	8 0
...	...		Kilrush ...dep.	725	10 0	11 0	130	5 0	5 0
...	...	4	Moyasta Junc.	740	....	1120	235	520	5 20
...	...	6½	Blackwier	750	flag	....	fl'g	...	...
...	...	9	Kilkee ....arr.	8 0	1035	1135	250	535	5 35

UP

UP	a m	a m	a.m.	a m	p m	p m	SUN p m
Kilkee ...dep.	...	7 25	...	11 0	...	5 0	5 0
Blackweir	...	flag	...	flag	...	510	5 10
Kilrush	...	7 25	...	11 0	...	5 0	5 0
Moyasta Jun...	...	7 45	...	1120	...	520	5 20
Doonbeg	...	8 10	...	1140	...	535	5 35
Craggaknock ..	...	flag	...	flag	...	fl'g	flag
Kilmurry	...	8 30	...	12 0	...	550	5 50
Quilty	...	8 35	...	flag	...	555	5 55
Millown M bay	...	8 55	...	1225	...	620	6 20
Lehinch	...	9 15	...	1250	...	640	6 40
Ennistymon	...	9 35	...	1 5	...	655	6 55
Willbrook	...	flag	...	flag	...	fl'g	...
Corofin	...	1010	...	1 45	...	725	7 25
ENNIS .....arr.	...	1035	...	2 0	...	750	7 50
Kilkee ...dep.	7 25	8 40	11 0	2 10	5 0	920	7 20
Blackweir	flag	flag	flag	flag	5 10	fl'g	7 30
Moyasta Jun.	7 40	....	1120	2 35	5 20	945	7 40
Kilrush..arr.	8 0	9 15	1135	2 50	...	100	8 0

Right:
West Clare Railway 4-6-0T No 1 *Kilrush,* built in Leeds by Hunslet in 1912. This was similar in design to the County Donegal engines of the same wheel arrangement. It is seen when new, its numberplate and date of manufacture standing out below the cab front. *LPC*

Bottom Left:
Timetable for the period commencing August 1900. *Paul Collins collection*

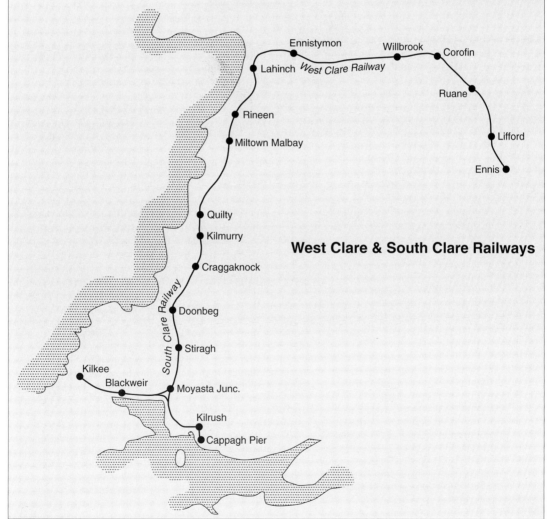

West Clare Railway

Ennistymon
Willbrook
Corofin
Lahinch
Ruane
Rineen
Lifford
Miltown Malbay
Ennis
Quilty
Kilmurry
West Clare & South Clare Railways
Craggaknock

South Clare Railway
Doonbeg
Stiragh
Kilkee
Blackweir
Moyasta Junc.
Kilrush
Cappagh Pier

this. However, the West Clare's decline was not as dramatic as elsewhere on the narrow gauge and there was talk of conversion to broad gauge. This was pretty fanciful, but the West Clare lasted long enough to be completely dieselised by CIE in the 1950s, the only instance of this happening in the British Isles.

In 1952 four Walker diesel railcars, virtually identical to the County Donegal Railway's Nos 19 and 20, which survive on the Isle of Man system, were bought by CIE for the West Clare and some new bogie carriages were provided to work with them. Three years later three 230hp Walker Bo-Bo locomotives arrived to complete the line's dieselisation, but sadly they could not halt the movement of traffic from rail to road and the West Clare network closed in February 1961.

There are plans to reopen part of it around Moyasta Junction. One steam locomotive, 0-6-2T No 5 *Slieve Callan* was preserved, mounted under cover on a plinth in the station

Top Left:
West Clare No 10 *Lahinch*. This was similar in design to No 1 but dates from 1903 and was built in Stoke-on-Trent by Kerr Stuart. With a tractive effort of 17,800lb, it was the most powerful engine on the line.
LPC

Centre Left:
A fairly short-lived West Clare engine was No 7 *Lady Inchiquin*. One of a class of three 0-6-2Ts built by Dübs of Glasgow in 1892, she was broken up in 1922; both her sisters outlived her by over 30 years. Perhaps the most curious aspect of the sisters was that their trailing wheels were of the same diameter as the driving ones. Harold Fayle, an authority on the West Clare, wrote that 'this was not done with any idea of having an eight-coupled engine, but only in the interests of standardisation'.
LGRP

Bottom Left:
No 8 *Lisdoonvarna*, another fairly short-lived West Clare engine. The line's first 2-6-2T, she was built by Dübs in 1894 and scrapped in 1925.
LGRP

yard at Ennis although in the late 1990s it was moved to Moyasta Junction, which is the focus of yet another scheme to revive part of the Irish narrow gauge. It was this engine, when I stood alongside it, that made me realise how very large a narrow gauge locomotive could be.

Below:
No 395, one of two Drewry petrol-engined railcars bought by the Great Southern Railway for the West Clare in 1928, a foretaste of things to come. A 30-seater, although just one occupant is visible in this picture, its running costs were 9d a mile. *LPC*

Below:
4-6-0T No 11, originally named *Kilkee*, built by Bagnall of Stafford in 1911, is seen in GSR days after its name had been removed. *LGRP*

Above:
4-6-0T No 3, originally named *Ennistymon*. It and No 7 *Malbay* were the last new steam engines built for the narrow gauge (other than for Bord Na Móna). They were supplied by Hunslet in 1922. It is seen here at Ennis with a brake van and two carriages. These latter are typical flat-sided, compartment type, six-wheelers. *LGRP*

Below:
Ennis in 1931. Behind the locomotive is the engine shed, while to the left are the carriage sidings. *LGRP*

Above:
4-6-2T No 1 at Ennistymon in the summer of 1931 with a train of two six-wheel carriages and a brake van, the latter with a 'birdcage' lookout in the roof for the guard. Ennistymon, described by Fayle in the May 1939 *Railway Magazine* as 'a prettily situated little town on the River Cullenagh, which here passes over picturesque falls,' was the last station on the line before the Atlantic coast was reached. It was the nearest station for Lisdoonvarna, a seaside spa popular with English visitors. *LGRP*

Below:
0-6-2T No 5c leaving Lahinch with an Ennis to Kilrush train. All West Clare engines had 'c' added to their numbers when taken over by the Great Southern in 125, at which time their names were also removed. Lahinch was the next station down the line from Ennistymon. Fayle describes it thus: 'One of the best-known watering places in the west of Ireland; its fame rests mainly on the well-known championship golf course but its other assets are the bracing air direct from the Atlantic and the picturesque cliff scenery in the neighbourhood… during the season there are frequent special excursions, a cheap "sea-breeze" trip being run from Limerick, with change of trains at Ennis, every Thursday.' The second carriage presents a rather extraordinary aspect with its towering clerestory roof. I got very excited one August day in 1975 upon coming across a sign at Lahinch which advertised rides on 'The world famous West Clare railway', only to discover it was a children's ride belonging to a travelling fair. *Real Photos*

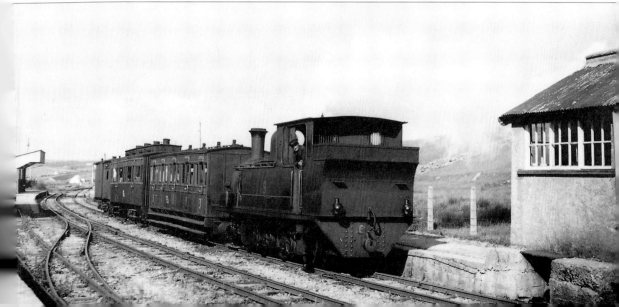

Above:
A close-up view of one of the West Clare clerestory carriages, taken in CIE days. No 33c is seen at Ennis on 22 April 1955. It appears to have corrugated tin sides and ends. Originally a 'tourist coach', it was divided into two sections, first and third, but by this late date had become all-third. *R. M. Casserley*

Below:
A first class, five-compartment, West Clare carriage, No 30c, seen at Kilkee, 15 July 1934. Lit by acetylene gas, each compartment seated six passengers. It was built in 1901. *H. C. Casserley*

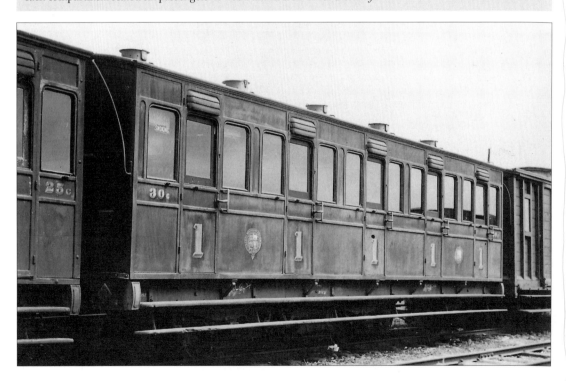

Above:
CIE made genuine efforts to keep the narrow gauge alive and in 1955 invested in three 230hp Bo-Bo diesel locomotives built by Walker Bros. Two of them, Nos F501/2, are seen newly delivered in Inchicore Works, before taking up work on the West Clare. *Seaton Phillips*

Below:
CIE also bought four railcars from Walkers, virtually identical to some supplied to the County Donegal. Ordered in 1952, they had power bogies similar to those fitted to the locomotives. With the arrival of the diesel locomotives, steam was ousted from all regular workings, freight and passenger. 2-6-2T No 2c is seen on one of its final workings at Lahinch on 28 June 1955, with railcar No 3386 at the other platform. *Peter W. Gray*

Above:
West Clare Walker railcar
No 3391, with one of the trailer
coaches built by CIE to run
with the diesels, poses in
typical Clare scenery.
Ian Allan Library

Left:
Ennis station in 1939, with the
broad gauge department to
the left and the narrow gauge
to the right.
LGRP

Above:
The same setting on a summer day in the 1950s. There is plenty of business for the narrow gauge in this animated scene, as passengers disembark from the broad gauge train on the left which has arrived from Limerick (a new steel-panelled carriage can be seen beyond the water column) and climb aboard railcar No 3390 and its trailer coach. *Ian Allan Library*

Below:
A few minutes later No 3390 is setting off for Kilrush, running alongside the broad gauge Limerick to Tuam line for about a mile before swinging westwards. *Ian Allan Library*

Moyasta, where the branches for Kilkee on the coast and for Kilrush on the Shannon diverged — a remote, windswept spot surrounded by bogland. On the right is the 1.50pm Ennis to Kilrush; on the left the connecting mixed train for Kilkee. Between them the station sign in standard bilingual CIE style. *C. P. Boocock*

Bottom Left:
The Kilrush terminus of the West Clare, with Walker railcar No 3388 and train in the station, with a handsome five-storey, granite warehouse forming a backcloth; 17 July 1957. *C. P. Boocock*

Above:
Kilkee, 7 June 1954, with railcar No 3387 alongside the main platform. *T. K. Widd*

Right:
Kilrush station in April 1994. The station itself is now a private residence. The warehouse sits beside a recently established marina for the increasing number of pleasure craft plying the Shannon. *Author*

Above:
Kilkee station, August 1975. Although turned into a private residence, the awning with its ornate iron columns is largely intact. The sea lies some half a mile away. *Author*

Below:
In a builder's yard in the town a short distance away were these six former West Clare covered wagons, minus wheels, in use as stores. Some still carried their metal numberplates. *Author*

12. Listowel & Ballybunion Railway

In County Kerry was that most peculiar of all Irish railways, the Listowel & Ballybunion monorail. Of course having only one running rail it did not have any gauge at all but it has generally been considered to belong to the narrow gauge camp, not least perhaps because its running rail was some three feet above the ground. Designed by the French Engineer Lartigue, it opened in March 1888 to connect the market town of Listowel, where the Great Southern & Western had a station on its line from Tralee to Limerick, to the resort of Ballybunion. Two guide rails, a few inches above ground level, helped stabilise the trains. One of its many curiosities was that each train ran with a set of steps marshalled somewhere in the middle, so that passengers could get from one side of the train to the other. Animals were placed at 90 degrees to the direction of travel, so that their weight was evenly balanced.

The Lartigue was a wonder in its time and certainly helped to popularise Ballybunion (visited in later years by more than one American President and possessing a magnificent beach and one of the world's top 10 golf courses) but it was far from efficient. Farmers would often leave crossings (designed like drawbridges) open, necessitating frequent stops to shut them, and if this was on the climb out of Listowel the little engines strained mightily to get restarted. It was far quicker to cycle and once motor vehicles arrived in Kerry, and buses and lorries appeared on the straight road between the two towns alongside which the Lartigue ran, then closure was a question of when rather than if. My father-in-law, a remarkably fit 95-year-old, says that travelling on the Lartigue always gave him a headache.

There were three locomotives, built by Hunslet: twin-boilered 0-3-0s, surely the only ones of this peculiar arrangement that the famous firm ever produced. The carriages looked almost conventional from the side but were actually in two halves, slung either side of the rail trestle. There were 13 of them originally, the first class seating 20, the third class 24. Ideally there needed to be a similar number of passengers on each side of a carriage.

Surprisingly perhaps, the Lartigue worked reasonably well and in its day was relatively prosperous. For the first three months of the 1907 summer season, for instance, 33,000 passengers were carried. The journey, with one stop at Lisselton Crossroads, took around 50min.

The fight for independence and then the Civil War saw a drastic decline in tourism, as well as actual damage to the line. This was enough to finish off the Lartigue, which closed in October 1924.

Below:
Timetable for the period commencing August 1900. *Paul Collins collection*

General Manager— P. MCARTHY.

LISTOWEL AND BALLYBUNION RAILWAY.

Miles.	DOWN.	WEEK-DAYS.				SUNDAYS.			UP.	WEEK-DAYS.					SUNDAYS.		
		a.m.	a.m.	p.m.	p.m.	p.m	a.m.	pm	pm		a.m.	am	a.m.	p.m.	pm	am	pm	pm	pm
	Listowel ..dep	8 5	10 30	1 0	4a30	9 b 0	10 30	3 0	7 35	Ballybunion d	6a10	9 10	11 45	3 0	7 0	9 0	1 30	6 45	8 30
4¾	Liselton	8 25	10 50	1 20	4 50	9 20	10 50	3 20	7 55	Liselton	6 30	9 30	12 5	3 20	7 20	9 20	1 50	7 5	8 50
9¼	Ballybunion a	8 45	11 10	1 40	5 10	9 40	11 10	3 40	8 15	Listowel ..arr	6 50	9 50	12 25	3 40	7 40	9 40	2 10	7 25	9 10

a 5.0 p.m. on Fridays and fair days.   *b* Saturdays only.   *a* Mondays only.

FARES.—Listowel to Ballybunion—Single, 1st class, 1s 4d ; 3rd class, 10d.   Return, 1st class, 2s ; 3rd class, 1s 3d.   Half these fares from or to Liselton.

Above:
Being a monorail the Listowel & Ballybunion had, strictly speaking, no gauge at all. However, I have always thought of it as firmly in the narrow gauge camp and so does my father-in-law, a sprightly 95-year-old who was brought up over the hill from it and rode upon it. So here it is. Locomotive No 3, built by Hunslet in 1888, poses with a number of well-dressed citizens at Ballybunion, sometime in the Edwardian era. *Author's Collection*

Below:
Another view of No 3 at Ballybunion, showing the hump in the tender necessitated by the raised centre rail, which gives it something of the air of an American Camelback. This is not entirely inappropriate as so many inhabitants of Kerry took themselves off across the Atlantic, which lies just beyond the terrace in the background, to find their fortunes. *LPC*

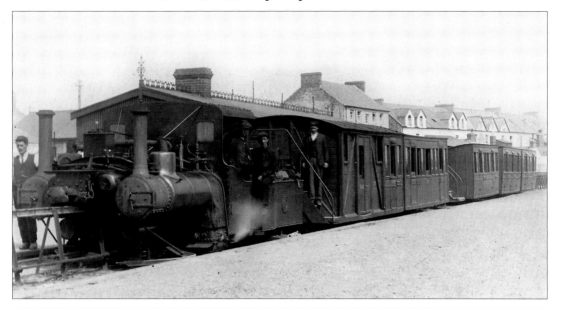

Above:
The inscription on the back of this print from the Ian Allan files is 'miscellaneous light', which certainly describes the unique Listowel & Ballybunion, or the Lartigue, to give it the name of its inventor and by which it is still fondly remembered. *LPC*

Below:
Some 20 years ago Cousin Mihall introduced me to Micky Barry, a farmer who lives at Lisselton, between Listowel and Ballybunion. Micky grew up fascinated by tales of the Lartigue. By patience and dedication, he has assembled together from pieces of scrap turned up by himself and others who farm along the route of the line, a section of the track and has even put together some sections of a carriage, including one of the large carrying wheels, just visible in the top left of the picture. He is holding one of the carriage maker's plates, Falcon Engineering of Loughborough. *Author*

13. Tralee & Dingle Light Railway

The Tralee & Dingle served, in the author's opinion, the most beautiful of all the beautiful western peninsulas. Opened in March 1891, it ran 32¾ miles from Tralee, the capital of the Kingdom of Kerry, through the sparsely populated bare hills between Tralee Bay and Dingle Bay to the fishing town of Dingle, with a six-mile-long branch from Castlegregory Junction (10 miles from Tralee) to Castlegregory.

Three 2-6-0Ts arrived from Hunslet's in 1889, ready for the line's opening. A Hunslet 0-4-2T for the Castlegregory branch came a year later; it lasted only until 1908. Three more 2-6-0Ts, this time from Kerr Stuart, were bought in 1902/3 and a sole Hunslet 2-6-2T was delivered in 1892. A final Hunslet 2-6-0T arrived in 1910. There were 21 bogie carriages and 77-bogie wagons, mostly cattle trucks.

Traffic was never overwhelming, the journey up hills and down valleys took around 2¼hr, depending on how many station stops were made; of the 13, most were conditional. There was a morning and an evening train in each direction, one including a portion for the branch, which also had one separate through service to Tralee. Cattle fairs kept the line in business.

Passenger traffic ceased in April 1939 and not even the outbreak of war ('The Emergency' in neutral Ireland) could revive it but the cattle fairs, which had supplied the line's backbone trade, kept it in business for goods. The monthly cattle fair at Dingle meant that one, sometimes two, long trains of cattle trucks would make their way eastward through the high hills. These specials attracted many enthusiasts from all over Ireland and from Britain. Eventually it all came to an end in June 1953.

Four locomotives were transferred to the Cavan & Leitrim and one survived that line's closure too, the sole 2-6-2T, No 5. Like so many Kerrymen, it was shipped off to the USA. However, it was not to remain in exile and in 1986 it returned home. By 1992 it had been restored to working order. Of all the Irish preservation schemes in various stages of progress, it is still the only narrow gauge steam engine to have once again taken up work on its old stamping grounds, running on the relaid section of the TDR between the outskirts of Tralee and Blennerville, where the Dingle Peninsula proper begins.

Manager—R. A. PARKES.	No Information		**TRALEE AND DINGLE RAILWAY**					AUG. 1900
DOWN.	WEEK-DAYS.	SUNDAY	**UP.**	WEEK-DAYS.	SUNDAY	
	a.m a.m acm p.m p m	a.m p m		a.m a.m a.m non p m	a.m p m	
Tralee ....d.	6 45 .... 1145	4 45 9 0	**Dingle** ....d.	7 35 .... 11c0 .... 3 45	.... 3 45	
Basin	6 50 .... 1150	4 50 9 5	Ballineesteenig	flag .... flag .... flag	.... flag	
Blennerville........	6 55 .... 1155	4 55 9 10	Lispole.............	7 55 .... 1120 .... 4 5	.... 4 5	
Tonavane	flag .... flag	flag flag	Garrynadur..........	flag .... flag .... flag	.... flag	
Curraheen	flag .... flag	flag flag	Puck Island	flag .... flag .... flag	.... flag	
Derrymore	flag .... flag	flag flag	Ballinosare..........	flag .... flag .... flag	.... flag	
Castlegregory Junct. a.	7 30 .... 1225	5 30 9 45	Aunascaul	8 29 .... 1150 .... 4 35	.... 4 35	
Do. d.	7 40 9 30 1235	5 45 10 0 5 45	Emalough	flag .... flag .... flag	.... flag	
Deelis...............	flag	flag flag flag	Glenmore	flag .... flag .... flag	.... flag	
Aughacasla...........	flag	flag flag	Glenagalth Bridge	flag .... flag .... flag	.... flag	
Castlegregory ....a.	8 15 10 0	1 5 6 15 1030 6 15	Castlegregory Junct. a.	9 20 .... 1245 .... 5 35	.... 5 35	
Castlegregory Junct. d.	7 35 .... 1245	5 41 9 50	Castlegregory........d.	7 08 45 .... 12 05 0 9 105 0		
Glenagalth Bridge	flag .... flag	flag flag	Aughacasla	flag .... flag	.... flag	
Glenmore	flag .... flag	flag flag	Deelis...............	flag .... flag	.... flag	
Emalough	flag .... flag	flag flag	Castlegregory Junct. a.	7 30 9 15 .... 1230 5 30	9 40 5 30	
Aunascaul............	8 32 .... 1 35	6 35 1058	Do. d.	9 25 .... 1250 .... 5 40	.... 5 40	
Garrynadur...........	flag .... flag	flag flag	Derrymore	flag .... flag .... flag	.... flag	
Ballinosare..........	flag .... flag	flag flag	Curraheen...........	flag .... flag .... flag	.... flag	
Puck Island	flag .... flag	flag flag	Tonavane	flag .... flag .... flag	.... flag	
Lispole..............	8 55 .... 1 55	7 3 1120	Blennerville.........	9 55 .... 1 20 .... 6 10	.... 6 10	
Ballineesteenig	flag .... flag	flag flag	Basin	10 0 .... 1 25 .... 6 15	.... 6 15	
Dingle ....a.	9 15 .... 2 15	7 20 1145	**Tralee** ....a	10 5 .... 1 30 .... 6 20	.... 6 20	

Note: SAT only (Down Sunday column); Saturday only (Up Week-days column); c Tuesdays, Thursdays, and Saturdays. Stop at Flag Station on signal.

Top Right:
Tralee & Dingle 0-4-2T No 4. This double-cab tram engine with its almost totally enclosed motion, built by Hunslet in 1890 for the Castlegregory branch, was unsuccessful and was scrapped in 1908. *LPC*

Below Right:
Tralee & Dingle No 2. This was one of the standard 2-6-0Ts built by Hunslet, of which there were six in all, although they were not identical and two were built by Kerr Stuart. There was also a Hunslet 2-6-2T. *LPC*

Bottom Left:
Timetable for the period commencing August 1900. *Paul Collins collection*

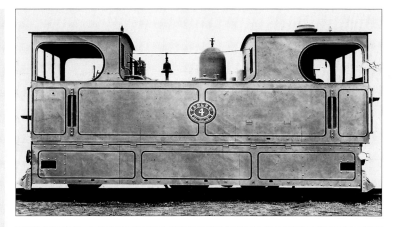

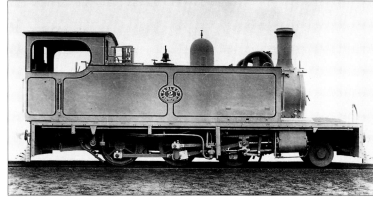

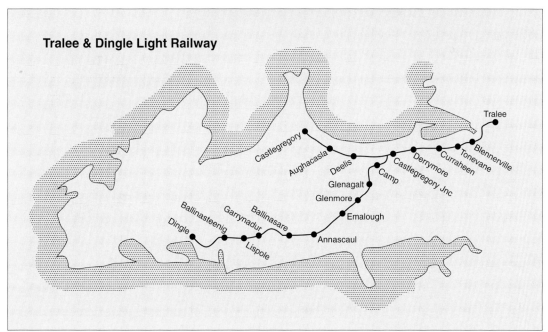

Tralee & Dingle Light Railway

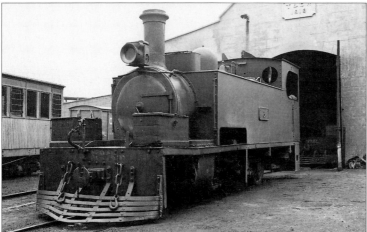

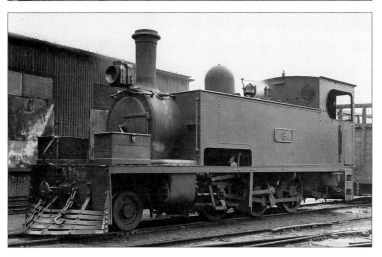

Top Left:
Tralee & Dingle No 4 over the inspection pit in 1939. This is a Kerr Stuart 2-6-0T, originally No 8 of 1903 but renumbered when the first No 4 was scrapped. *LGRP*

Centre Left:
No 3, one of the original 2-6-0Ts, outside Tralee sheds in 1931. Note the inscription over the shed entrance. *LGRP*

Bottom Left:
Another view of No 8. All Tralee & Dingle locomotives were fitted with cowcatchers, for the track ran for much of its length alongside the main road through the Dingle Peninsula and sheep regularly strayed across it. For similar reasons the engines sported powerful acetylene headlamps at the base of the chimneys. *LGRP*

Top Right:
A pair of Tralee & Dingle locomotives at the Dingle end of the line. *Ian Allan Library*

Centre Right:
Tralee & Dingle brake third No 24T, 14 July 1934. All the line's carriages and wagons ran on bogies. Seats in third class were unupholstered. *H. C. Casserley*

Bottom Right:
Composite carriage No 18T. The doors opened inwards. Seats were arranged partly along the length of the carriage and partly crosswise. *H. C. Casserley*

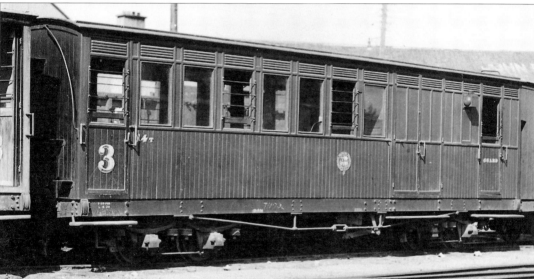

Left:
Tralee & Dingle 2-6-0T No 1 running through the streets of Tralee, 24 August 1951. It has just come from the interchange sidings after taking on coal in the broad gauge yard. The narrow gauge station was several hundred yards to the west of the broad gauge one.
Author's collection

Centre Left:
Passenger traffic ceased in April 1939 — the bus between Tralee and Dingle town took less than half the time of the trains — and regular goods traffic ended in March 1947. However, cattle specials continued to run until June 1953 and in their final years attracted much interest. There is no finer scenery in all of Ireland than in the Dingle Peninsula and this undoubtedly contributed to the line's attraction. No 8 — note the crudely painted number on the buffer beam — approaches Dingle.
Real Photos

Bottom Left:
No 8 leaving Annascaul with steam to spare, 29 June 1951.
Real Photos

Right:
Nos 1 and 2 blast their way up the 1 in 29 out of Lispole, 28 July 1951. *W. G. Aspell*

Below:
A couple of English enthusiasts watch Nos 1 and 2 passing Annascaul.
Real Photos

Above:
Inevitably the surviving locomotives were not in the best of condition in their final years. Nos 8 and 2 are seen in difficulties with a long line of cattle trucks on the steep gradient near Puck Island, 25 August 1951.
Ian Allan Library

Centre Left:
The former Tralee terminus of the Tralee & Dingle Railway.
Author

Bottom Left:
No 5 heads towards the familiar hills of the Dingle Peninsula in August 1993.
Author

Above:

The Tralee & Dingle shares with the County Donegal the distinction of having come back from seeming permanent extinction, to be worked once again by its original motive power. Upon closure of the T&D, 2-6-2T No 5 was transferred to the Cavan & Leitrim, and when *that* was closed it was shipped across the Atlantic to be preserved in New Hampshire. However, like so many more recent Irish migrants, it was eventually able to return, when a section of narrow gauge line was relaid from the outskirts of Tralee to Blennerville, the first station out. It steamed again in 1992 and is seen here back at work in County Kerry. *Author'*

Right:

No 5 with its train of two Spanish-built carriages at Blennerville. *Author*

14. Cork & Muskerry Light Railway

The first section of this line, between Cork Western Road and Blarney, eight miles distant, opened in August 1887. Next came the 9½-mile Donoughmore branch in May 1893, and finally the 11-mile extension to Coachford. One might have thought that the world-famous tourist attraction of Blarney Castle would have pulled in the punters but the GSWR got there first, its station being on the main line out of Cork, and the Cork & Muskerry always struggled financially.

Its motive power was varied, although all of it was four coupled. Giving an engine the name *Blarney* seems to have been the kiss of death. The first Blarney, a Kitson 0-4-2T dating from 1888, was the first CMLR engine to be sold off, while the second, a Hunslet 4-4-0T, was possibly the shortest-lived narrow gauge engine in the entire country. It arrived in 1919 and was scrapped by the Great Southern a mere eight years later. The rest of the fleet comprised three Falcon 2-4-0Ts of 1887, later rebuilt as 4-4-0Ts;

two Falcon 4-4-0Ts built as such in 1898 and 1904; and two Green 0-4-4Ts of 1892/3. Carriage stock consisted of 26 bogie vehicles.

The line closed on the last day of 1934. No rolling stock is known to have survived.

Top Right:
Blarney, one of the original Cork & Muskerry locomotives, Kitson-built 0-4-2Ts of 1888. An underpowered little thing, it was sold out of service in 1910. *LPC*

Centre Right:
Its replacement was a far more substantial-looking affair. This is the second *Blarney*, also No 4. Far and away the most modern locomotive on the line, its career was nevertheless even shorter than its predecessor, for it lasted a mere eight years, being broken up by the GSR in 1927. Built by Kitson's, a company favoured by many Irish — and other — narrow gauge companies, one wonders just why its life was so short. *LPC*

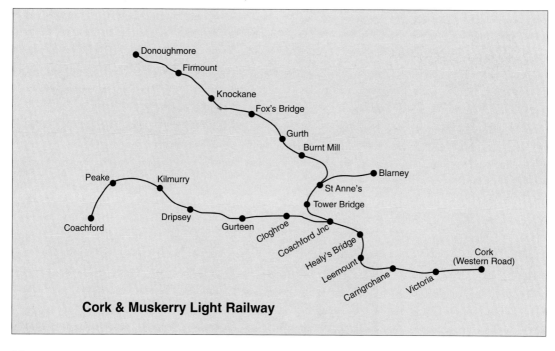

Cork & Muskerry Light Railway

Right:
Cork & Muskerry 4-4-0T No 7
Peake. It was just two years old
when this picture was taken at
Cork in 1900. Built by the
Falcon Engine Co, it lasted
until the end of the line in
December 1934.
LGRP

Left:
As this picture clearly shows, the Cork & Muskerry ran for much of its length alongside roadways. Like other similar lines, this proved its downfall but when this picture was taken in 1900 few people in Ireland had seen a motor vehicle. This heavily loaded eight-coach train is carrying excited excursionists to one of the great Irish tourist attractions, then as now, Blarney Castle.
LGRP

Top Left:
Pair of Cork & Muskerry open wagons. *LGRP*

Centre Left:
Cork & Muskerry 0-4-4T No 5K leaving the Cork Western Road terminus on 15 September 1929, its train consisting of a couple of standard, rather handsome, matchboard-sided bogie carriages. No 5K was one of a pair built by Green of Leeds in 1892 and originally named *Donoughmore*. It was standard, rather unimaginative, Great Southern practice to remove names from the locomotives it inherited. It did, however, deign to provide one of its standard station nameboards, even though it closed the line within nine years of acquiring it. *H. C. Casserley*

Above:
No 6K arriving at Cork Western Road, c1930. *Author's collection*

Below:
No 6K standing on the turntable at Western Road on the same day, although the fact that it has arrived bunker-first does not suggest that engines were regularly turned at the end of each run. *Author's collection*

15. Cork, Blackrock & Passage Railway

This line was unusual among narrow gauge railways in Ireland (or indeed anywhere in the British Isles) in that it was essentially a suburban commuter line. The CBPR ran for its entire 16-mile length along the western shores of Cork Harbour.

It opened in June 1850 as a broad gauge line running from Albert Street, Cork, to Passage, 6½ miles distant. It was converted to 3ft gauge in 1900, extended to Monkstown in 1902, Carrigaline in 1903, and Crosshaven in 1904. It was single track with passing loops, except for two miles of double track between Albert Street and Blackrock, the only such section on the Irish narrow gauge.

Its four locomotives, Neilson Reid 2-4-2Ts, looked as though they had been intended for suburban commuter traffic in England and converted to narrow gauge configuration as an afterthought. The summer-only 35min nonstop run between Crosshaven and Cork, which they handled with ease, was one of the fastest schedules anywhere on the narrow gauge. They operated with the line's fleet of 28 bogie compartment carriages.

Despite the CBPR's smart running, electric trams gradually took away much of the railway's Cork to Blackrock traffic, the closure of the Haulbowline Dockyard was a further blow, and buses delivered the *coup de grâce*. The Crosshaven to Monkstown section closed in June 1932, the rest three months later.

All four locomotives were transferred to the Cavan & Leitrim, two surviving until the end of that line in 1959.

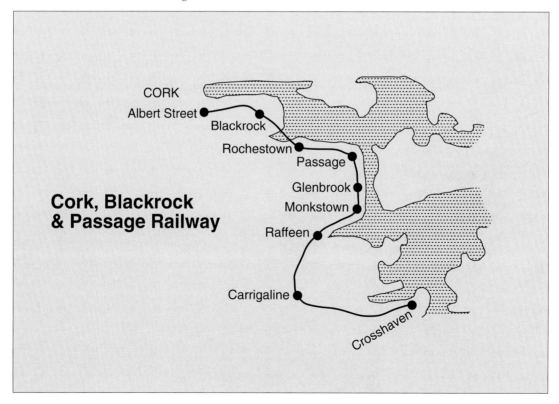

Cork, Blackrock & Passage Railway

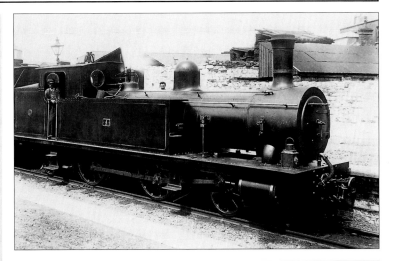

Top:
Timetable for the period commencing August 1900.
Paul Collins collection

Right:
In its narrow gauge days (it was converted from broad gauge in 1900) the Cork, Blackrock & Passage Railway standardised on Neilson Reid 2-4-2Ts. There were four of them; this is No 4. As they never had names, the Great Southern was not able to remove them. Viewed from the side they had a very lanky appearance with well spaced out wheels and looked rather more broad gauge than narrow. The diameter of their driving wheels, four and a half feet, was the largest of any Irish narrow gauge engines and they were in effect standard gauge suburban tank engines modified to work on the 3ft gauge. *LPC*

Bottom Right:
This is the first train on the Crosshaven extension, opened in 1904. It brought the total length of the line to 16 miles. There were virtually no gradients and the entire journey was alongside Cork Harbour. *LGRP*

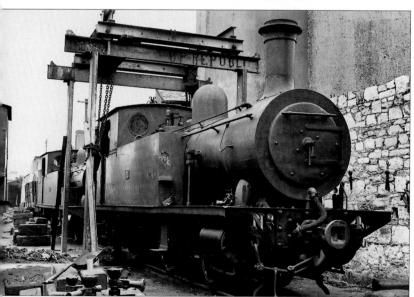

Above:
Cork, Blackrock & Passage 2-4-2T No 7P (GSR numbering) approaching Cork, 10 June 1932.
H. C. Casserley

Left:
No 4P plus two of the other three 2-4-2Ts at Cork in 1931.
LGRP

Above:
No 7P leaving the Albert Street terminus of the CBPR line on 10 June 1932. The section between Monkstown and Crosshaven had closed 10 days earlier and the remaining eight miles would close in three months' time.
H. C. Casserley

Below:
The GSR obviously thought highly of the CBPR 2-4-2Ts, for all were transferred to the Cavan & Leitrim line. They were renumbered 10L-13L. No 11L was scrapped in 1936 but the rest survived into the 1950s. One of them is seen at work on the Cavan & Leitrim section c1953. *J. J. Dowling*

15. Schull & Skibbereen Railway

(West Carbery Tramways & Light Railway Co)

The most southwesterly railway in Ireland, this 15-mile County Cork line opened in September 1886, running around the shores of the evocatively-named Roaringwater Bay from Schull to Skibbereen. At the latter it connected with the Cork, Bandon & South Coast Railway's Baltimore branch.

There were two trains a day in each direction, usually mixed, with a third for the tourists on summer Sundays. The journey took around 80min, so it was no wonder that the Schull & Skibbereen eventually succumbed to road competition. The wonder was it lasted as long as it did.

Below:
Timetable for the period commencing August 1900. *Paul Collins collection*

SCHULL & SKIBBEREEN TRAMWAY & LIGHT RAILWAY. [Manager— Mr. T. CREEDON.

Miles	DOWN	WEEKDAYS		Singl Fares		Miles	UP	WEEK-DAYS		Singl Fares	
		p a m	p m	1	3			a m	p m	1	3
				s d	s d					s d	s d
	SKIBBEREEN ...dep	12 20	6 30	s d	s d		**SCHULL** ....dep	9 15	4 0	s d	s d
4	Newcourt	12 33	6 43	0 6	0 3	2	Woodlands.............	9 25	4 10	0 4	0 2
5	Church Cross	12 40	6 50	0 8	0 4	5	Ballydehob...........	9 45	4 30	0 10	0 5
6	Hollyhill..........	12 50	7 0	1 0	0 6	8	Kilcoe	10 0	4 45	1 4	0 8
7	Kilcoe	12 55	7 5	1 2	0 7	9	Hollyhill..............	10 5	4 50	1 6	0 9
10	Ballydehob........	1 15	7 25	1 8	0 10	11	Church Cross..........	10 15	5 0	1 10	0 11
13	Woodlands ......m	1 30	7 40	2 2	1 1	12	Newcourt	10 22	5 7	2 0	1 0
15	**SCHULL**.........arr	1 40	7 50	2 6	1 3	15	**SKIBBEREEN** ......arr	10 35	5 20	2 6	1 3

On Thursdays a Special Train leaves Skibbereen at 8-30 a.m. for Ballydehob and Schull, returning at 10-30 a.m. from Schull. A Special Train leaves Schull at 6-0 a.m. on Skibbereen Fair Days. On Thursday the 9-15 a.m. will not run ; a train leaves instead at 6-30 a m On Schull and Ballydehob Fair Days a Train leaves Skibbereen at 6-0 a.m. a Starts on Saturdays at 1-0 p.m.

Schull & Skibbereen Tramways & Light Railway

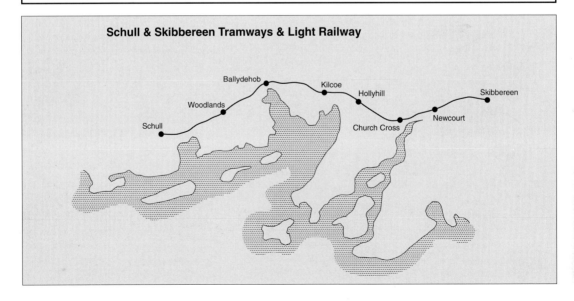

The original motive power consisted of three Dick Kerr tramway type 0-4-0Ts, which were not very successful, 'pitching like a ship in choppy water,' to quote A. T. Newham, and were restricted to 15mph. Indeed so useless were they that the line had to shut down until they could be made to function a little more successfully. Eventually, in 1888, a Nasmyth Wilson 4-4-0T was obtained, two more similar engines, but built by Peckett of Bristol, arriving in 1905 and 1914. The tram engines were all scrapped by 1926. Eight carriages, four bogie and four 4-wheelers, sufficed for passenger traffic. In 1936 an 0-4-4T arrived from the Cork & Muskerry to replace one of the life-expired 4-4-0Ts.

While World War 2 prolonged the life of a number of narrow gauge lines, it had the opposite effect on the Schull & Skibbereen. Fuel shortages in 1944 brought about a temporary closure that April. It reopened in November 1945 but the extension of the Cork-Skibbereen bus service to Schull was a death-blow and, coupled with another fuel crisis in the severe winter of 1947, led to the last passenger train running on 27 January 1947. The line was officially closed in September 1952.

Below:
Schull & Skibbereen (West Carbery) 4-4-0T No 1 *Gabriel* at Ballydehob in 1933. *Gabriel* — for some reason the GSR has forgotten to take away its name — was built by Peckett in 1905. It was scrapped in 1937. *Real Photos*

Above:
Ballydehob Viaduct and
station in 1918.
Ian Allan Library

Left:
The viaduct at Ballydehob in
1996. *Author*

Top Right:
Four-wheel wagons and
carriages at Schull, 1 July 1938.
H. C. Casserley

Bottom Right:
Schull station, beside
Roaringwater Bay, in 1996.
Author's collection

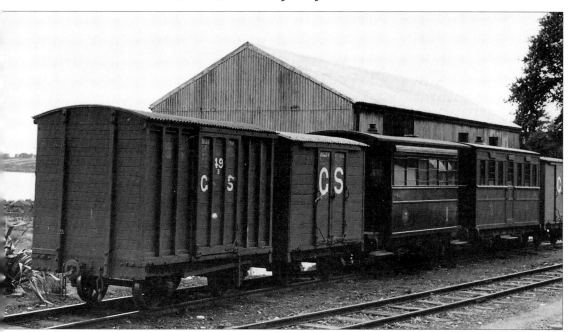

Other Railways

Glenariff Mineral Railway

Nearby to the Ballymena, Cushendall & Red Bay Co Railway, the four-mile-long Glenariff Mineral Railway opened from a pier at White Arch on the Antrim Coast in 1873 to serve local mines but their failure meant the end of the railway. It closed in 1885, the first Irish narrow gauge line to do so. It never carried passengers but its two locomotives and wagon fleet were bought by the Londonderry & Lough Swilly Railway.

Annaghmore Turf Railway

Owned by the Irish Peat Development Co, this 3ft line opened in 1907 to serve the peat bogs and a factory near Maghery on the southern shores of Lough Neagh, Co Armagh. Eight miles long, it was originally worked by two Belfast-built electric locomotives dating from 1907 and known locally as 'travelling hen-houses'. They took their current from an overhead electric cable fed from the company's peat-fired power station. In its latter years it was diesel worked, the electric locomotives having been replaced in 1957.

Upperlands Horse Railway

This quarter-mile 3ft gauge line was opened in 1900 to serve the linen factory of William Clark & Sons Ltd, at Upperlands, Co Londonderry. There was a station here on the broad gauge NCC Antrim to Macfin line.

Always horse worked, although a Ferguson tractor was also used in latter days, bales of linen were transferred from narrow gauge bogie wagons of approximately one ton capacity to NCC wagons for export all over the world via Belfast.

Haulbowline Admiralty Railway

A network of 3ft 6in gauge lines was opened to serve construction works at the British naval base in Cork Harbour. Two Aveling Porter four-wheeled gear tank engines were delivered in 1875 and 1878. A permanent 3ft 6in gauge railway, with nearly three miles of track, replaced the construction lines and a Manning Wardle 0-4-0ST was delivered in 1897. After the Irish Free State took over Haulbowline, there was little need for the railway and it ceased to work around 1930.

Baldonnel Aerodrome Railway

This 2ft gauge line was opened to help in the building of this RAF base. It ran for some 2½ miles from Lucan South station on the GSWR main Dublin to Cork line. To work it, two Hudswell Clarke 0-6-0WTs arrived early in 1918. Apart from conveying building materials, the construction workers themselves were carried on the railway each morning, having connected with a broad gauge train from Kingsbridge, and were brought back in the evening. The line closed with completion of the aerodrome in 1919.

Glenfarne Forestry Line

This 2ft gauge line was in existence for around a year in 1919 and conveyed timber over a distance of some three miles to Glenfarne SLNCR station, County Leitrim, for transfer. Two engines were used, a Hudswell Clarke 0-6-0WT, identical to the Baldonnel Aerodrome Railway ones, and another, unidentified, smaller one. With the end of tree felling the railway fell into disuse and the locomotives were eventually sold for scrap.

Mullaghmore Barytes Railway, County Sligo

Another 2ft gauge line, this was seven miles long and opened in 1928 to link the mines owned by Barium Consolidated Ltd with Mullaghmore Harbour. It was worked by a curious Simplex petrol engine built in Bedford. The driver sat sideways, so that his machine could travel in either direction without him

Top Left:
No 3 waits to head off to the shores of Lough Neagh on the now closed privately-operated Shane's Castle Railway. Its tiny 2ft driving wheels seem scarcely large enough to support its own weight and are quite dwarfed by its substantial copper-capped chimney and commodious cab. *Author*

Centre Left:
Before the various preservation schemes, it was Bord Na Moná, with its extensive network of lines across the Midland peat bogs, which kept the narrow gauge alive. A train loads up from one of the massive turf-cutting machines at Clonsast on the Bog of Allan in 1972. *Author*

Below:
A train in the charge of a Ruston 48hp diesel locomotive receives attention. In the distance is Portarlington power station, fed by turf from the bog. *Author*

having to change his seating arrangements. The line operated for some three years but various factors, including the worldwide depression following the Wall Street Crash, brought about its end and all the railway material was sold in 1935.

The Marconi Railway

A 1¼-mile line was built across boggy swampland in 1906 to the 2ft gauge, to serve the pioneering wireless station set up by the famous Italian-born scientist (his mother was Irish) near Clifden, County Galway. Construction of the wireless station would have been impossible without the railway. A Dick Kerr three-ton 0-4-0ST was the motive power. In 1919 the first men to fly the Atlantic, Alcock and Brown, crash-landed close to the railway. The wireless station was wrecked during the Civil War of 1922-3, technological progress meant that there was no need to rebuild it, and so the days of the railway came to an end too.

Irish Industrial Minerals Co, Achill Island

Achill is yet another of those remote, remarkably beautiful western peninsulas or islands in which Ireland specialises and which was briefly served by a railway. In this instance it was a 2ft gauge line which operated from 1910 to 1916 in connection with a whitestone quarry. It ran between the quarry and Keel Quay. Two locomotives were used: *Derwent*, an 0-4-0T built by Orenstein & Koppel of Berlin, and *King George*, a Bagnall 0-6-0T.

Fergus Reclamation Scheme

A 2ft 6in line operated in connection with land reclamation south of Clarecastle in County Clare. Hunslet provided an 0-4-0ST, *Fergus*, in 1881, chiefly remembered in local folklore on account of falling into the river after which it was named, presumably overcome by uncontrollable homesickness. The driver and four others went into the river too but all survived, *Fergus* being recorded back at work two months later. Severe storms hampered the reclamation work and *Fergus* was sold in 1883 and was next seen at a quarry in Warwickshire. However, another reclamation scheme began in

the 1890s. This time the gauge of the railway was 600mm. The locomotive was an Andrew Barclay 0-4-0ST delivered in 1893. The reclamation scheme continued for some 50 years but, although a section of the line was horse operated into the 20th century, the locomotive had gone before 1900.

Bianconi Farm Line

A rather remarkable one-mile-long, 2ft gauge railway operated between 1910 and 1929 on the farm owned by John Bianconi, the grandson of the pioneer of Irish stage coaching, at Lacknashannagh, County Clare. Some of the wagons and track came from the Fergus Reclamation Scheme but the locomotive was a unique machine, best described in the words of Walter McGrath as 'like a road steam lorry running on rails'. It was built in England but its maker is not recorded. Bianconi was a highly ingenious engineer but declining health brought about the railway's neglect and its components were sold off after his death in 1929, the 'rail lorry', which had cost £380 when new, going for £2.10s. Its new owners, a religious community in County Limerick, never managed to get it shipped across the Shannon and it gradually rotted away.

Shannon Scheme, Ardnacrusha

An undertaking almost unimaginably vast by the standards of every other industrial scheme we have so far looked at, was the hydro-electric one on the Shannon, north of Limerick City, which was constructed between 1925 and 1930. Two extensive railway networks were set up: one of 900mm, one of 600mm. The locomotives, of which there were no less than 93 on the former network and 13 on the latter, were all 0-4-0Ts. There were also two electric locomotives which worked a short length of the 900mm railway. All were of German manufacture from various makers. The railway was operated by Siemens Bauunion. Over 3,000 wagons saw service on the scheme which, when complete, provided electricity for the greater part of Eire. Everything was shipped in from Germany and when the work was completed it was all shipped back again. Walter McGrath recalls that 'By 1931 there were no signs of the system left.'